PUBLICATIONS OF THE UNIVERSITY OF MANCHESTER
No. CCIII

FRENCH SERIES
No. V

TENNYSON IN FRANCE

Published by the University of Manchester at
THE UNIVERSITY PRESS (H. M. McKechnie, M.A., Secretary)
23 Lime Grove, Oxford Road, Manchester

TENNYSON IN FRANCE

BY

MARJORIE BOWDEN, M.A.

MANCHESTER UNIVERSITY PRESS
1930

MADE IN ENGLAND
All rights reserved

FOREWORD

As far as is compatible with logical grouping, I have in this essay maintained a chronological order, as keeping most nearly to reality.

To Professor Orr, of Manchester University, at whose suggestion this study was first undertaken, and who has always given it his warm support; to Professor Paul Hazard, of the Sorbonne, under whose help and encouragement the book grew; to Professor Charlton, of Manchester, for much helpful advice; and to my husband for his untiring help, I wish to express my very sincere gratitude.

MARJORIE BOWDEN

Manchester, 1929

CONTENTS

	PAGE
FOREWORD	v
INTRODUCTION	1

CHAP.
- I. EARLY CRITICISMS 7
  - I. First Impressions 7
  - II. First Judgments of Tennyson as Poet Laureate 18
- II. THE GREAT CRITICS 24
  - I. Taine 24
  - II. Montégut and Scherer . . . 33
- III. GROWTH OF TENNYSON'S REPUTATION—ADAPTATIONS AND TRANSLATIONS, 1850–1875 . . 42
- IV. FORTUNE OF THE LONGER POEMS UNTIL 1892: TRANSLATIONS OF THE "IDYLLS OF THE KING", "ENOCH ARDEN", AND "MAUD" . . 59
- V. THE EVOLUTION OF CRITICISM: THE PRE-SYMBOLIST CRITICS 84
- VI. TENNYSON AND THE SYMBOLIST MOVEMENT . 100

CHAP.		PAGE
VII. Review and Readjustment	. . .	129
I. Tennyson's Death	. . .	129
II. Biographies	. . . .	135
III. Translations	. . . .	138
IV. Centenary Opinions	. . .	144
Conclusion		149
Bibliography		155
Index		163

INTRODUCTION.

It is doubtful whether the figure of Tennyson has yet found its true place in the literary perspective. The giant of Victorian days has dwindled, but repeated attempts to estimate him show how uncertain his real stature still is. He can still arouse curiosity and fierce differences of opinion. He has survived the first violent reaction. "We smile to-day at our Victorians", says Mr. Harold Nicolson, "not confidently, as of old, but with a shade of hesitation; a note of perplexity, a note of anger sometimes, a note often of wistfulness has come to mingle with our laughter".[1] Tennyson has passed into history. His philosophy, his modes of thought, were perishable; his art may well be enduring. It is useless to rail at the idol, now that the idol has fallen. The Poet Laureate is dead; what remains is to judge the poet.

It may be worth while to hear an impartial opinion, assessments which are disinterested even when hostile. Let us try to see Tennyson through the eyes of the French, or, rather, in the highly polished mirror of French literary criticism.

Tennyson, more than any other poet, gives the impression of being British to the core. So faithful did he remain

---

[1] *Tennyson: Aspects of his Life, Character and Poetry*, London (Constable), 1923. See also A. C. Bradley, *The Reaction against Tennyson*, 1917 (Essays by members of the English Association, No. 39); Hugh I'Anson Fausset, *Tennyson: A Modern Portrait*, London (Selwyn & Blount), 1923; and Alfred Noyes, *Some Aspects of Modern Poetry* (Tennyson and some recent critics), London (Hodder & Stoughton), 1924.

in all things to the British point of view, that he might never have left his native island. Yet he travelled frequently, although he never had any intimate knowledge of the countries he visited. He went to France several times, always as a tourist. In 1861 he travelled in the Pyrenees and in Auvergne, where "the foul ways and unhappy diet overset" him; in 1864 he made a literary pilgrimage to the country of King Arthur, whom he had just celebrated in his *Idylls*. He found among the Bretons little enthusiasm for the Celtic legends, although at Lannion, when it became known that he was the poet of King Arthur, his landlady refused to allow him to pay his bill. He spent some days in Paris with Locker-Lampson in 1862, visiting the Louvre and the churches, strolling on the boulevards, grumbling from his seat at the Théâtre Français that he felt as if "stuck on a spike in Hell". The next year he was at Rheims. He was back again in Paris in 1872 and 1874, reading with pleasure the poetry of Hugo and Musset, admiring at the Théâtre Français the art of Got, the Coquelins, and Mlle Reichemberg. A last stay at Pau in 1875 gave him the opportunity of exploring the Pyrenees, the part of France which appealed to him, perhaps, more than any other.[1]

These travels made their impression on him, but one gathers from his notes and correspondence that he was always glad to be home again. He is struck by "the sensible look of the people of London". Truly, he believed, as he writes in *Hands all Round*:

> That man's the best cosmopolite
> Who loves his native country best.

[1] For details of all these journeys, see Hallam, Lord Tennyson, *Tennyson: A Memoir by his Son*, London, 1897 (Macmillan), 2 vols. (vol. i. pp. 472-476; vol. ii. pp. 5, 67, 77, 114-115, 157, 159, 211).

He was interested in French literature, and had opinions of his own on his French contemporaries. He preferred Musset to Hugo, in whom he saw "an unequal genius, sometimes sublime", who reminded him that there is only one step from the sublime to the ridiculous. His friendship with Hugo seems to have been a very perfunctory affair, hung on the slight pegs of Hugo's hospitality to his son Lionel. Tennyson's lack of sympathy appears even in the sonnet to Hugo written on this occasion: "Victor in drama, Victor in romance", which, as Edmund Gosse observed, lacked tact in monumental proportions.[1] Of Parnassian poets he knew only Coppée and Jean Aicard.

His early poems reveal dislike and contempt for France; Nelson and Wellington were no legendary heroes to him, Napoleon was a "ravening eagle". His allusions to France; "whom martial prowess only charms", to war, "this French god, this child of Hell", or "the red fool-fury of the Seine", show that he shared the prevailing English mistrust of French unrest. Later on, he came to understand French political life better. Hallam, Lord Tennyson, tells us that, especially after the Franco-German War, his father was "filled with admiration at the dignified way in which France was gradually gathering herself together".[2]

In these personal dealings of Tennyson with France there is obviously little to prepossess the French public in his favour. He was not already known in literary circles like Moore: he did not rebel against respectability like Swinburne, or die gloriously in exile like Byron. There was nothing sensational in his serene and moral life, mellowing to ripe old age in the solitudes of Farringford and

---

[1] *Mercure de France*, April 1904, pp. 69, 70, Edmund Gosse: *L'Influence de la France sur la poésie anglaise.* Victor Hugo's characteristic answer to Tennyson is quoted in the *Memoir*, vol. ii. p. 218.

[2] *Memoir*, vol. i. p. 344.

Aldworth. His personality remained aloof: his work stood entirely on its own merits in France.

That work is not of a kind easily appreciated by a foreigner; and this for two reasons. It is, as we know, the pure expression of the mind of a Victorian Englishman. Even ignoring the undercurrent of Gallophobia in his early patriotic poems, we find throughout his work that insular complacency which rouses foreigners to fury. The patriotic poems are splendid examples of *morgue britannique*—Swinburne called them "beardless bluster, reminiscent of a provincial schoolboy". Throughout, his work breathes the air of England, of that England which few in France could know. For the untravelled he is more often than not the poet of what stands for England in their minds—"sweet home", *jeunes miss*, clergymen, and maiden ladies.

Secondly, Tennyson defies translation, as most of those who translated him into French are ready to admit. Tennyson himself considered that "French is a poor language for translating English poetry". Hence, the works best known in France are those simplest in form—*Enoch Arden* and the *Idylls*—poems in blank verse which have a story to tell. Except to those who have what Mallarmé called *l'ouïe anglaise*, the real Tennyson is not revealed. Who could translate

>   Willows whiten, aspens quiver,
>   Little breezes dusk and shiver
>   Thro' the wave that runs for ever . . .

or

>   unhailed
>   The shallop flitteth silken-sailed
>   Skimming down to Camelot?

The real Tennyson, lord of language, whose words

often follow one another with the inevitableness of some great symphony, the Tennyson of *The Passing of Arthur* or of *Tears, idle tears*, is seen as through a glass darkly in translation. The freshness and colour of his poetry fade and become insipid, the imagery passes through the mill of French precision and suffers in the process, the characteristic and evocative compound words of Tennyson's invention are watered down into lame explanatory phrases. Naturally, when the glamour is gone, the faults lie bare, so that in France critic after critic accuses Tennyson of coldness, over-elaborated elegance, unoriginality of thought. These charges are no doubt all too true, but they are less obvious to Englishmen, for whom Tennyson's word-pictures have their full power, to whom it seems that not a few of his lyrics are part of themselves.

Much has been written in France about Tennyson. French criticism was aware of him almost from the beginning (1833), and was still discussing him at the time of his centenary and even after. We shall try to determine whether he was more read about than read. His work never became the object of a literary vogue, was never even translated in full. Interest in him never worked up to enthusiasm; it fluctuated in somewhat remarkable fashion over a long period. Yet, each time discussion is renewed, we feel that his work is better understood. As his long career is followed step by step, each stage being marked by notices, studies, and chosen translations in reviews of authority, we are conscious of a growing readiness among French readers to know more about this most English of poets. After early disparagement, due largely to lack of comprehension, his work gradually wins the admiration and affection, if not of the public at large, at least of a goodly body of cultured readers. Soon, perhaps too soon, he becomes a "classic": his name is found in the programmes for *baccalauréat*, *licence*, and *agrégation*: numerous annotated editions appear, in which the moral lessons of his life and work are dwelt upon for the edification of French youth. But such a tribute to his art is not quite to the purpose of this essay, which is to trace the history of Tennyson in France from a purely literary point of view; and to show, firstly, to what extent and in what quarters Tennyson's work gained appreciation in France: to follow the development of that appreciation; and secondly, to determine what part Tennyson played in the forming of the French poetic outlook towards the end of the century.

CHAPTER I

EARLY CRITICISMS

I. *First Impressions*

EVEN in the earliest French criticisms of Tennyson it is interesting to find a new point of view. Knowing little about him, frankly making use of what had been written in England, French critics did not hesitate to form an independent opinion. We are conscious at once that Tennyson is being examined according to intellectual and psychological standards very different from those of his own country. French critics are all the more at their ease inasmuch as Tennyson is still quite obscure, and criticism in England is far from unanimous about him.

Poems, Chiefly Lyrical (1830), were welcomed by enthusiastic articles from Arthur Hallam and Leigh Hunt; but these were really exceptions. John Stuart Mill wrote approvingly of the new poet in the *Westminster Review*, emphasising his metaphysical methods and attaching him to the utilitarian school. The publication of the *Poems* of 1832–1833 drew down on the protégé of the utilitarians the raillery of Christopher North in *Blackwood's*; the *Quarterly* dissected the poems in a tone of heavy irony which was meant to crush them out of existence.[1] We find the repercussion of all these ideas in France.

[1] *Westminster Review*, Jan. 1831, pp. 210-224; *Blackwood's Magazine*, May 1832, pp. 721-741; *Quarterly Review*, Jan. 1833, pp. 81-96.

With the exception of a bare announcement in the *Journal de littérature étrangère*, 1827 (vii. p. 113), of *Poems by Two Brothers*, Tennyson is first introduced to France by the enterprising but short-lived *L'Europe littéraire*.[1] Two anonymous articles which appear on the 6th and 15th of March give a clear and intelligent account of the nature of Tennyson's art. The critic has no doubt borrowed his information from the *Westminster Review*: he sees in Tennyson "a young man from the ranks of the utilitarian school, brought up among the followers of Bentham, who has cherished the idea that the Benthamite philosophy—with its axioms, corollaries, and dogmas, with its oracular and abstract style—need not prevent him from being a poet". But he is not satisfied with a second-hand opinion. In Tennyson's poetry he finds a most subtle expression of the Northern temperament, quite foreign to the genius of the Latin races; coldly penetrating thought is here brought to bear on the most intense and passionate of life's happenings; the result does not lack greatness, depth, or variety; yet it has something quite outside the comprehension of Southern intelligences. In spite of obvious faults, of which not the least is affectation of style, Tennyson is a true poet. The critic goes so far as to say that it is Tennyson who seems most fitted to succeed Byron—praise, indeed, on the lips of a Frenchman of 1833, though expressed with a touch of malice: "The mob of poetasters that had sought to share the heritage of Lord Byron has retreated before the new Benthamite

---

[1] This interesting journal did not survive for a year—March 1, 1833–February 7, 1834. It was at first published in folio three times a week. Mr. Palfrey, whose thesis deals with *L'Europe littéraire*, attributes these articles to Baron d'Haussey, who was in England at this time, and who a month later wrote for this journal the account of an interview with Sir Walter Scott.

poet. Tennyson may possibly fill up the gap left by the death of Childe Harold. We do not give him out to be a complete genius: but of all the versifiers to whom the easiness of English rhythm and prosody opens up such a broad and inglorious path, he is the only one who, since the death of the great man, has given proof of any original power."

The second article attempts a closer study of Tennyson (March 15, pp. 29, 30). Eight verses of *Recollections of the Arabian Nights* are quoted with a free translation in prose, which, while keeping a certain oriental flavour, conveys neither the warmth of colour nor the bright imagery of Tennyson's poem. A much happier choice is the *Death of the Old Year*, quoted to show how Tennyson finds poetry in the most ordinary things of life. The translation of this poem is simple and accurate.

This critic's judgment of Tennyson is thoughtful and comprehensive. He notes in him a predilection for things of the past, he admires the ease with which Tennyson moves in the realms of fairy-tale and history, his gift of distilling beauty from the humblest aspects of life, and of catching by intuition and observation the most delicate and fleeting impressions. He saw, in fact, most of the possibilities of Tennyson's art. We shall see that for a long time yet such French reviews as deign to notice Tennyson's existence merely deal with him in the rank and file of young poets. *L'Europe littéraire* is alone in considering him worthy of a somewhat detailed study at this moment.

The *Revue de Paris*, for instance, limits its activities in English poetry to publishing a letter from an alleged Englishman calling himself Sir John Perriwig, who belittles all contemporary English poetry and sighs for the golden days of Elizabeth. Modern poets are the basest of imitators: Tennyson deserves special mention because he is the most shameless of all. "M. Tennyson's poetry is full of the most obvious imitations. . . . He is naturally apt to mistake bombast for strength, and silliness for simplicity. . . . His philosophy is merely incomprehensible mysticism; his sensibility is as clumsy as German sentimentality; his love poems, which ought to be simple, are elaborately pretty. His muse languishes, rolls her eyes, swoons away, etc. etc., like some coquettish old maid." Thus are the subscribers of the *Revue de Paris*,[1] at least, warned against the impostor.

An interesting example of an independent French opinion is to be found in the *Revue des Deux Mondes*,[2] where a French critic annotates and amplifies a short study of contemporary English poetry by Allan Cunningham. It is a pity that these notes, which leave less than a third of the page for the original article, are anonymous: for their writer shows sounder judgment than the English poet. He considers that there is a certain banality about the compliments kindly distributed by M. Cunningham to his colleagues in the art of poetry. From a host of names he picks out Tennyson and Elliott as the most prominent poets. Cunningham credits Tennyson with a strong and pleasing imagination, but regrets that the originality of his thought is often marred by deliberate peculiarities of diction. The sentiments which he seeks to express do not always spring naturally from the subject

[1] *Revue de Paris*, April 1833: *La Semaine de Du Bartas*, p. 5. On Tennyson, pp. 7 and 8.

[2] *R.D.M.*, Nov. 1833, Allan Cunningham: *Histoire biographique et critique de la littérature anglaise depuis cinquante ans* (1784–1833), 2nd article, p. 396. The *R.D.M.* mentions the annotator as one of its soundest critics of English literature. The names of Amédée Pichot and Xavier Marmier suggest themselves.

under his hand. Cunningham adds that many English critics look to Tennyson for the future of English poetry. The French critic is less cautious: "there is no comparison between Tennyson and the foregoing versifiers. He is original: a metaphysical poet without mysticism, passionate yet capable of analysing, full of faults, strength, and thought: a bearer of new ideas". The two books of the young poet excel those of his contemporaries *"pour la profondeur et la verve"*. Cunningham is of opinion that criticism is crushing poetry: our commentator reminds us that criticism did not paralyse Byron or Southey or Moore, and that poets like Tennyson and Elliott, who give voice to a popular feeling or a new idea, soon hold the attention of the public.

A somewhat superficial article of the *Voleur* (Dec. 20, 1834) tries to throw a new light on Tennyson. Instead of seeing in him a poet of syllogisms and deductions, it represents him as a disciple of Moore, dwelling on his exoticism, which, like his master's, is "rather exaggerated and wearisome". This critic finds nothing but praise for the delicacy of feeling in Tennyson's portraits of women, and attempts a translation of *Eleänore*. "We are afraid lest our pen should rend its light and airy tissue", he says, and his fears are only too well grounded. He skips difficulties and makes free use of commonplace expressions:

I watch thy grace. . . .	Tu me parais le chef-d'œuvre de la beauté humaine.
I muse as in a trance the while Slowly, as from a cloud of gold, Comes out thy deep ambrosial smile.	Dans quelle extase me jette ton sourire céleste et rayonnant!

Edward FitzGerald pointed this article out to Tennyson as France's first impression of him, adding that it would make him laugh.

Between 1833 and 1842 Tennyson, mourning the loss of Arthur Hallam, and discouraged by criticisms of his early poems, kept silent and allowed himself to be forgotten. Naturally, during these nine years, little attention is paid to him in France. In 1839 Philarète Chasles, reviewing the English literature of the day, speaks of Tennyson as if his little hour of fame were over once and for all. He persists in calling him the Homer of the Benthamites, destined to sing the greatest good of the greatest number. A critic of the Romantic school, he deplores the metaphysical trend of Tennyson's poetry: "Tennyson's rhythm, otherwise bold and strong, was sorely hampered by those chains; the mechanism of his laboriously skilful versification increased the constraint forced on him by a conventional philosophy.... Thus the great luminaries of poetry die out, thus light and heat disappear behind a veil of finespun conceits": a funeral oration to which Tennyson fortunately gave the lie.[1]

Philarète Chasles protests against this poetry, which he does not understand, and which does not agree with his ideas of taste. To him, Tennyson's verse is one more example of a fatal tendency in Northern poetry, already typified in Spenser and Shelley: "formless reverie, impotent analysis, sterile subtlety.... A certain fascination draws one towards this kind of enjoyment, which seems to combine purity and loftiness; but one soon begins to miss the sound governing and concentrating force of art."

[1] See *R.D.M.*, March 1, 1839, pp. 583-608, Ph. Chasles: *De la littérature anglaise actuelle.* See also *R.D.M.*, Feb. 1, 1841, pp. 456-457: *Revue littéraire et critique de la littérature anglaise.*

Meanwhile in England Tennyson's work had made its way underground; the revised edition of his poems, issued in 1842, had an immediate success. Henceforward his fame steadily grew.

In France, one review at any rate condemned the alterations. *L'Écho de la Littérature et des Beaux-arts*[1] considered that the poems had been "*singulièrement tronquées, dénaturées, allongées*". "It is really extraordinary", runs the comment, "how far the tactless suppression of a few expressions has robbed these charming verses of their beauty." The *Revue britannique*, on the other hand, remarks that in Tennyson's view originality is evidently not incompatible with diligence and method (Aug. 1842, p. 389).

It was the volumes of 1842 which brought Tennyson to the notice of the *Revue britannique*, which followed more consistently than any other in France Tennyson's rise to fame. This review let the poems of 1830 and 1833 pass unnoticed, and in June 1838 declared that poetry in England was in a transition stage: "the thunder of Byron rumbles only in the distance now, and the new poet has not yet appeared". Between August and October of 1842 the translations of a dozen poems of Tennyson appear in the *Revue britannique*. Henceforward this review, under the editorship of Amédée Pichot, is constantly publishing translations of Tennyson, and commenting in the *Correspondance politique et littéraire* on the details of the poet's life and popularity.[2] These frequent allusions,

[1] *Écho de la Littérature et des Beaux-arts en France et à l'étranger* (in 8vo, Paris, 1840–1848), 1842, p. 270.
[2] Amédée Pichot died in 1877. In 1883 (Dec., p. 489) this review which had discussed Tennyson so much, refers to "Tennysson, l'auteur de '*La Princesse Maure*'": and after 1887 makes no further mention of Tennyson.

giving as they did a prompt and generally accurate idea of English criticism, did much to make Tennyson known.

The first translations—in August 1842—are anonymous, and in prose. Amédée Pichot points out in a note that English critics are unanimous in praising Tennyson's *verve* and originality, qualities which are best studied in his more personal poetry. For purposes of translation, it has been found advisable to deal with the simpler poems, of ballad or legend form. To this prudent choice we are indebted for simple and adequate translations of *Dora*, *The Lord of Burleigh*, *Saint Simon Stylites*, *Saint Agnes' Eve*, *Godiva*, and *Ulysses*. The second attempt was less successful. Readers had expressed a wish to have a more poetic rendering of the new poet's verse. Apologising for a venture at once bold and timid, the *Revue britannique* published a translation in French verse of six of the more characteristic poems.[1] Whether the charm of these poems, *où l'Indécis au Précis se joint*, was not fully understood, or whether the translator was not good enough for his job, these translations are mostly, for all their goodwill, travesties. To begin with, the translator takes liberties with the text, omitting or amplifying as he thinks fit. Generally, it is the evocative or imaginative words which he omits, whilst his amplifications are astonishingly unnecessary:

---

[1] Oct. 1842, p. 346, anonymous translations of:
The Poet (Le poète).
Lady Clare (Lady Clare et Lord Ronald).
The Sisters (Les deux sœurs).
Circumstance (Un tableau).
Love and Death (L'Amour et la Mort).
Audley Court (Le dîner sur l'herbe).

EARLY CRITICISMS

. . . but ere night we rose
And sauntered home beneath
    a moon, that, just
In crescent, dimly rained
    about the leaf
Twilights of airy silver. . . .
        (*Audley Court*)
        ad finem.
	Allons, dis-je à Francis, voici
	    l'ombre du soir.
	Place au doux rossignol, et
	    rentrons au manoir.
	Nous avons encor loin de ces
	    lieux au rivage,
	Et nos mères déjà doivent rêver
	    naufrage.
	Nous partons: par bonheur,
	    le lumineux croissant
	Sur les arbres bientôt jeta ses
	    rayons d'argent.

The Poet is so distorted that it is scarcely recognisable—

With echoing feet he threaded
The secretest walks of fame:
The viewless arrows of his
    thoughts were headed
And winged with flame,
Like Indian reeds blown from
    his silver tongue.
	Sur les monts, sur les flots,
	    pour nous quand tout ré-
	    sonne
	Comme un murmure ou
	    comme un bruit,
	Pour nous quand l'oiseau
	    chante et l'insecte bour-
	    donne
	C'est un langage qu'il traduit.

Better attempts are made at simpler poems such as *Circumstance* and *Love and Death* and the French version keeps something of the directness of the ballad *The Sisters*. But *Lady Clare* is acclimatised by means of little eighteenth-century pastoral touches of which Tennyson never dreamed. Lord Ronald calls her his *bergère*, and asks suspiciously, "*Serait-ce ce berger Lubin Qui vous attend dans la prairie?*" This is, all things considered, a not very successful endeavour to show the diversity of Tennyson's poetry, but praiseworthy inasmuch as it is by far the earliest attempt of its kind.

    The *Revue britannique* follows up Tennyson's growing

reputation, noting successive editions in London, marvelling to find such admiration for a poet who is *loin du matérialisme de cette capitale positive*, commenting on the poet's love of seclusion, or recording the award of a pension to him by Peel. Quotations from *The Mermaid* and *Lady Clara Vere de Vere* even appear in the journal's dramatic criticism.[1] Amédée Pichot, in his *Excursion dans le pays de Galles et en Irlande*, calls attention to the *Morte D'Arthur*, "a fragment which has certainly the style and colour of the days of chivalry" (Jan. 1845).

Thus Tennyson's name becomes familiar enough to the cultured public for the *Revue des Deux Mondes* to consider him worth a study. This article, by E. D. Forgues, appeared in 1847 (May 1). Its tone is entertaining. Tennyson's reputation was steadily growing in England, but he was not yet pre-eminent. Hence Forgues, writing for the most conservative public in the world, felt safe in allotting a brief and circumscribed renown to this *rimeur étranger*.

"Old Nick", as he often styled himself, was more at home as a critic of the novel. Even in this article he cannot refrain from comparing Tennyson and Dickens. Certain aspects of the early Tennyson he represents well enough. He gives a good range of examples of Tennyson's art, from *Mariana* to *The Two Voices*: the competent translations show that he is familiar with his texts.

Yet we feel the writer's entire lack of sympathy for his subject. We are aware of two widely different and irreconcilable standards of taste. Forgues cannot forgive Tennyson for his sudden transitions from dream to reality, he is irked by "a profusion, often incoherent, of all kinds of images". Only by an effort does the writer master his

[1] *Chronique littéraire*, April 1844, p. 487; Oct. 1847, p. 441.

EARLY CRITICISMS

irritation in order to present a fair summing-up of Tennyson's powers.

According to Forgues, Tennyson represents the tradition of Wordsworth carried on by Shelley and Keats: his poetry finds its inspiration in *"ce monde surnaturel, ce microcosme intérieur que chaque imagination se crée"*. Poetry thus conceived may, Forgues admits, be exquisite, but it allows too much liberty to individual caprice, eludes all translation or interpretation, becomes the possession of a select few, and can never pretend to universal or lasting fame. Tennyson is so preoccupied with formal beauty that his verse comes near to being purely plastic art. "Take the voluptuous melody and the skilful archaism from his poetry, and at once you do it irreparable harm, for the simple reason that Tennyson is a creator only in details of style." The poet's thought is hazy with vague benevolence, gentle resignation. He is merely a passive spectator of life, and as a philosopher, null. The real worth of his poetry is to be sought elsewhere. In his landscapes, which are fresh and delicate like those of Constable, Tennyson shows himself a true artist: he reveals "a soul on which the aspects of nature leave a real and profound impression, a mind which has received from God the rare and sublime power of transmitting them to a whole race".

Forgues dismisses Tennyson's poetry as unlikely to have any influence abroad, least of all in France. Finally his irritation gets the better of him, and the Frenchman, with impressive orthodoxy, perorates. Nobody will deny to the fellow-countrymen of Racine, he protests, a due sense of harmony: nor imaginative power and a liking for poetical abstractions to the nation that could admire Chateaubriand and the brilliant poets that followed him. Yet the French mind, while ready to make the largest

C

concessions to airy independence, vague fancy, and melodious caprice, will always keep that integrity, that precision, that love of a complete meaning and of full light on things which preserve it from the heady raptures of the German or British muse. "An epithet which, though dazzling, is incoherent and ill-adapted to the word it is meant to colour, the odd juxtaposition of two jarring words, the sham grandeur of some half-hidden image, the attempt to achieve the sublime through excessive *naïveté*, the disproportion between a solemn tone and a trivial subject, will never create as much illusion among us as among our neighbours."

Tennyson thus provokes an attack on the artistic ideals of the North from a writer who was by nature incapable of understanding them; and although opinions on his work are fairly defined, his reputation suffers from this lack of understanding which, as we shall see, persists. At the start, the notion of Tennyson as a metaphysical poet was much exaggerated. His poetry was far from being appreciated as mere poetry. French critics were too anxious to classify it, to judge it by intellectual standards.

II. *First Judgments of Tennyson as Poet Laureate*

The year 1850 brought two important events in Tennyson's life—the publication of *In Memoriam* and his appointment as Poet Laureate.

In France, where no such office exists, the name of Laureate does nothing for Tennyson's reputation but give it stability. Some of the daily papers indulge their wit at the expense of this official singer to Queen Victoria: even more serious critics mention with malice the pension of £100 a year and the butt of malmsey. But henceforward Tennyson is the representative poet of England, and criticism, whether hostile or not, must take him seriously.

The *Revue britannique* hastens to greet the new laureate —"truly a nightingale in the melody of his song and in his love of solitude".[1] Joseph Milsand, in the course of a long study which is the first isolated apology of Tennyson, welcomes him as representing what is newest and most characteristic in English poetry.[2] For Milsand, contemporary English poets are in the van of modern thought. France, together with the rest of Europe, has remained indifferent to the successors of Byron, believing them to be weaker varieties of the same species, whereas with Tennyson and Browning English poetry has left behind the Byronic attitude of revolt and has risen to a plane of serener thought. Their verse, for all its maturity, keeps its spontaneity and imaginative power. Especially is this so with Tennyson, whose verse is peculiar in its mingling of freshness and mellowness. In *Locksley Hall*, for example, the passion that inspires Tennyson is as strong as Byron's, but his instrument includes a new octave, that of conscience. It is the same moral preoccupation which makes *In Memoriam* great. "I say deliberately that I do not know a book which leaves one with a more tremendous idea of human nature. The conceptions of certain thinkers give us a glimpse of infinity in the capacities of the mind. Tennyson's book gives us a glimpse of infinity in the moral faculties. One could make this book one's Bible."

Tennyson, says Milsand, thinks in *a parte*. Thought, with him, precedes inspiration. Then the forces of thought,

[1] Nov. 1850, p. 225.
[2] R.D.M., July 15, 1851. This article, with a further essay on *The Idylls of the King*, is republished in *Littérature anglaise et philosophie*, Paris (Fischbacher), 1893.

so to speak, are withdrawn, revealing themselves as the guides only of his imagination. "Like the ground after a summer shower, he sends towards heaven emanations from all that is within him. These vapours go to form an inexhaustible poem, composed as it is of mirages, allegories, and transfigured recollections."

For Milsand, Tennyson's style approaches the ideal. Everything—images, cadences, colour, rhythm—is subordinated to the needs of the theme. His constant aim is harmony, appropriateness; he has a conscience, where taste is concerned. One feels that this is not only a personal conviction, but a reply to those who accuse Tennyson of banality of thought and over-elaboration of style. A generous critic, Milsand has only one reproach for the poet. He is too brief: he is incapable of sustained effort. But if the strings of his instrument soon cease to vibrate, says Milsand, it is to that that they owe their sweetness, and they respond again to the gentlest breath of inspiration.

Neither so generous nor so well-informed, a critic of the *Revue contemporaine*[1] sees in the nomination of Tennyson a sudden veering round of public favour, which he puts down to the dread of having any gaps in the continuity of English literary glory. Tennyson's poetry, much criticised at first, he says, now finds favour probably because there is nothing better. Tennyson is only a tempered, prudent, and disillusioned Lakist, whose only care is the slow elaboration of beautiful verse.

The *Revue de Paris*,[2] summing up twenty-five years of English literature in a few pages, has not time to go very deep. On the subject of Tennyson, the critic hashes up

[1] L. Étienne, *Revue contemporaine*, 1853, vol. vi. (Feb.-Mar.), p. 205.
[2] *Revue de Paris*, Sept. 1854: *Esquisse d'un tableau de la littérature anglaise, 1830-1854*.

stale opinions. Forgues had said: "*Considéré comme penseur, comme philosophe, Tennyson retomberait dans la foule.*" The echo of 1854 gives back: "*Comme penseur et philosophe, Tennyson est complètement nul.*" Tennyson is an abstractor of quintessences, representing a school of poets who, without youth or energy, are a weariness to the spirit; he is a retrograde poet, not to be thought typical of the nineteenth century, the era of hope and progress.

In Memoriam offers a further temptation to the hasty critic. This long sequence of poems, written in a uniform measure, poignant and monotonous as grief itself, with its subtleties and obscurities of thought and expression, dismayed those to whom the English language offered any difficulty. One feels that judgments on this poem, more often than on any other, are second-hand. Of all Tennyson's work, *In Memoriam* is the poem which has evoked the most widely differing criticism. It is a kind of touchstone: by his judgment of *In Memoriam* we can tell how far a critic understands Tennyson, how far he has troubled to understand him.

The form is new. The *Revue britannique*, finding it hard to define, is non-committal. "A mournful work, full of feeling", runs the comment, "a series of epitaphs or elegies in honour of a dead friend, in which it is fair to say that there are good and even admirable lines" (June 1850, p. 437).

We have seen that Milsand, as befitted a friend of Browning, was not disconcerted by the obscurities of *In Memoriam*. He is not one of those who dismiss the poems as concetti: he is struck by their perfect sincerity and moral force. Here are no heartrending cries, no convulsions of grief, he says, and even in his feverish moments we are conscious of the poet's robust moral health. Superficial critics, on the other hand, find the poem incredibly, incomprehensibly dull; "nobody ever thought of expressing his grief for a dead friend in such a skilful and methodical fashion as Mr. Tennyson", says L. Étienne, who is irritated by this slow sculpture of verse. Of this impatience we shall find one notable example later on; but eager supporters of *In Memoriam* are not far to seek among the anglicists in French criticism.

Maud, likewise, was not easy work for the critics. It is curious that at first it is neither the psychological novelty nor any lyric beauties in the poem which attract attention, but the bellicose tirades which form its prologue and epilogue. The *Revue britannique*, always prompt, expresses astonishment that this dreamer and maker of sweet songs should take to blowing the war-trumpet. The critic considers it a triumph to have expressed this strange and melancholy theme, these ravings of a hero of melodrama, in beautiful verse. But this is not Tennyson's real vein: his genius appeals to the tender-hearted and to lovers of romance; it would be a pity for him to desert the poetry of sentiments and ideals for the sounding brass of the war-clarion.[1]

L. Étienne, on the contrary, admires this new aspect of the graceful and melancholy poet of the *Princess* and *In Memoriam*. He hails Tennyson as a worthy son of Tyrtaeus, the poet of warriors whom spleen drove to battle, and considers that the English public is wrong to regret this new theme of their idyllic poet. His invectives may be wrong, but his feelings are right.[2]

Something of the disconcerted attitude of Tennyson's English admirers is found in an article by Arthur Dudley

[1] *Revue britannique*, Sept. 1855, pp. 234-236.
[2] *Revue contemporaine*, April 1, 1857: *Les Poètes de la guerre en Angleterre.*

in the *Revue des Deux Mondes*.[1] *Maud* is judged to be the work of a poet who is past his best: it lacks sincerity, and has not the vigour of *In Memoriam* or *Locksley Hall*. Tennyson has not fulfilled the promise of his youth. "We must reproach Tennyson for his lack of that sense of the immutable which rises above present impressions . . . he is swayed by passing emotions, is drawn along by them instead of being their master."

Maud is no longer able to shock readers by its violence of expression and looseness of form. We overlook those of its qualities and defects which drew most comment on both sides the Channel. We are indulgent towards the crudeness of the melodrama, we can almost forgive the malignant stupidity of its chauvinism for the sake of those lyric passages which shine like gold among the faded tinsel.

Until now we have had to marshal scattered and fragmentary opinions about Tennyson. It is only with the greater names that a sense of order and proportion enters. Emile Montégut, so distinguished as a critic of our literature, had barely entered upon a study of Tennyson's now considerable work when another and greater critic triumphantly anticipated him.

[1] Feb. 15, 1856: *La Poésie anglaise depuis Shelley.*

CHAPTER II

THE GREAT CRITICS

I. *Taine*

TAINE set out to write not only a history of English literature but a study in national psychology. In 1860, when his opinions, based on his reading, had already taken definite shape, he came over to England to verify his impressions of the nation which he had undertaken to portray for the benefit of his countrymen. His stay lasted some ten weeks. On his return to France he published in the *Journal des Débats* articles on his contemporaries—Carlyle first of all, then John Stuart Mill, and, as soon as he comes to poetry, Tennyson. Taine, who has a high opinion of English poetry, chooses Tennyson among the poets of his day as most worth study. In the fourth volume of the author's *Littérature anglaise*,[1] Tennyson alone represents contemporary poetry.

Taine's logical and scientific criticism presents a clear and striking image of the poet, but it is of necessity incomplete. At the time when Taine wrote, *Enoch Arden* had not appeared, nor poems such as the *Grandmother* and *The Northern Farmer*, nor yet the dramas. Yet Taine adopts a somewhat final tone, and his criticism of Tennyson

[1] The study of Tennyson consists of three articles which appeared in the *Journal des Débats*, April 3, 4, and 6, 1861. They were reproduced in full in *L'Histoire de la littérature anglaise* (tome iv. chap. vi.), 1864.

leaves a deep and lasting impression in the minds of those who have to be satisfied with ready-made ideas of foreign literature.

With one serious exception this is a masterly study, giving proof of a solid knowledge of Tennyson's poetry, and of much understanding. There is in it no national prejudice. But prejudice there is. Taine is over-logical. Bent on discovering, in any work he studies, an essential unity, he assumes every artist to be impelled by a *"faculté maîtresse"*, which dominates his whole work. With Tennyson, this dominant note is an amiable dilettantism.[1]

Taine, knowing Palgrave to be an intimate friend of Tennyson's, questioned him about the *milieu* in which Tennyson wrote his early poems. Taine would like to have found that this delicate poet had been a pleasure-seeker, living in a house full of rare bibelots and exquisite works of art. Palgrave succeeded in convincing the great critic that Tennyson's early life, as one of eleven brothers and sisters in a country parsonage, had not been that of a sybarite, and reluctantly Taine had to give up the idea of Tennyson the dandy.

But dilettante he remains, for Taine. The early poems reveal natural dilettantism: *In Memoriam* is a failure because its theme does not suit a dilettante: *Maud* and *Locksley Hall* give glimpses of violent feeling that the public resents in a dilettante: the *Princess* and the *Idylls* mark his return to a most definite and yet delightful dilettantism. Such is Taine's point of view. It may be true in the main. Even if it were not, such logic would carry conviction.

In the first article *Son Talent* Taine shows us Tennyson through the eyes of his English public. He makes subtle

[1] See R.D.M., Sept. 15, 1862: *Les précurseurs et les chefs d'école.*

use of the pronouns *on* and *nous* which it is amusing to disentangle. In a few rapid strokes we are shown Tennyson as a poet who has the great quality of coming at the right time. After the storm and stress of romanticism Tennyson's poetry has all the advantages of a quiet sunny evening. Leaving the work of his predecessors, charged as it is with sentiment, imagination, and revolt, we come upon Tennyson's, and find it exquisite. We find in him all the ideas and rhythms which had charmed men of late, but in him they are purified, tempered, uttered in matchless style. He ends an age. In what had stirred others he proceeds to find enjoyment.

Taine admires the delicacy and grace of Tennyson's portraits of women, in which each word is like a touch of colour which cunningly sets off the touch next to it, and in which we discover a delightful mingling of audacity and refinement, a refinement which leads him at times into affectation or even preciosity. Taine shows us the poet making his excursions into nature or history, free from all prejudice and unruly passion, picking and choosing here and there, satisfied with what he can perceive and taste, and enjoy. One found enjoyment with him, says Taine, one was charmed with his real or imagined landscapes (we must mistrust this pronoun *on*). One let oneself be carried away by the music of Tennyson to languorous lands like the shore where the companions of Ulysses, contented dreamers like the poet himself, forgot their fatherland and gave themselves up to indolence.

Taine analyses Tennyson's dilettantism and sees in it a double current. Not only is Tennyson a dilettante by temperament, but his public forces this attitude upon him and will not allow him violent feelings. Yet a fiery core of passion burned beneath the smooth surface of his verse, and now and again, in his poems on Nature and love, some vivid line lights up, as with a flash of colour, his staid and correct design. In the temperament of every true poet, observes the critic, there is a constant renewal of sensibility, a rapture born of contact with the forces of Nature and the passions of man, which are the beatings of Nature's heart. "And Tennyson felt them; not always, but twice or thrice at least he dared to utter them. In *Locksley Hall* we find the sincere accents of overflowing emotion, and hear the voice of a man." Taine here speaks for himself, and not in the name of the British public lulled into agreeable reverie. *Locksley Hall* is strong and courageous. *Maud* is even more so; the poem vibrates with energy, hence its unevenness, its unreserve, its violence. The poet, hitherto so correct and reticent, confesses himself, seems to think and even weep aloud. He no longer sings, but talks, in the loose, bold style of ordinary conversation; and "poetry here flowers magnificently, as in fact it does flower in the midst of all our vulgarity". Thus Taine understood and admired the power of *Maud*; he attaches no importance to its truculent passages. As an outburst of feeling, the poem was to remain unique. Discouraged by the hostility of the public, Tennyson *rentra dans son azur*. He resumed his languid elegance. Taine does not seem to regret this submissiveness. "He was quite right. He was better off there than anywhere else."

It is curious that a critic who can so appreciate *Maud* cannot or will not understand *In Memoriam*. In an article on the study of English literature, Taine writes of Tennyson and Meredith: "Above all, one must like them: sympathy is always the first source of understanding".[1]

[1] Taine has borrowed this axiom from Carlyle (*On Heroes*), and quotes it in his study of Carlyle.

It is precisely this sympathy which is lacking in Taine's judgment of *In Memoriam*. He is irritated, and perhaps disconcerted by the poem. The few sentences in which he dismisses it are unworthy of the great critic. His contempt for it is not necessarily a lapse of literary taste; there is a lapse of taste, a breach of courtesy, in the expression of his contempt. "*In Memoriam* is stiff, dull, and too skilfully arranged. He is in mourning, it is true, but he wears it like a well-bred gentleman, with brand-new gloves, wiping his tears with a cambric handkerchief; during the religious service which completes the ceremony he displays grief expected of a respectful and well-drilled layman."

Of all the French critics who wrote on Tennyson, Taine, the greatest, is alone in thus attacking *In Memoriam*, and his attitude brought many reproaches upon him. Swinburne, who was certainly not biassed in Tennyson's favour, takes up arms to defend him against this "foreign champion who strikes with the sharp point of his lance the spotless shield which bears the words '*In Memoriam*'." In Swinburne's opinion, Taine misses the mark. In his impatient dismissal of the poem Taine did not grasp its real weaknesses, one of which, to Swinburne, is its parade of modesty—"its ostentatious modesty, its pretentiously unpretentious philosophy".[1]

Taine, logical and convinced, sees simply a poignant theme handled in a dilettante fashion, and does not realise that this poem hides under its reserve more sincerity than *Maud*. *In Memoriam* once relegated to a lower plane, Taine returns to his first Tennyson, for whom reality is neither beautiful nor pure nor harmonious enough, and who is only at his ease when in his own gracious realm of fantasy and chivalric legend. There is, first, *The Princess*, which

[1] See *Fortnightly Review*, clxx., 1881.

Taine finds delightfully English, in the tradition of Shakespeare and the Renaissance. He sees in it an abundance and almost a surfeit of youthful vigour: it is an overflowing of his imagination and his emotions. The poet plays with beauty, and no jesting could be more tender nor more whimsically romantic than this. Taine does not even recognise the nineteenth-century argument thinly disguised in the theme of *The Princess*. "Here Tennyson thought and felt", he says, "like a young knight of Renaissance days." He accepts the *Idylls of the King* with the same good faith. They were not for him the Idylls of Albert the Good. It never enters his head that these fifth-century knights were Victorian. "Tennyson has revived, with admirable art, the spirit and the language of these old legends. This time he is epic, archaic, and naïf like Homer and the old *trouvères* of the *Chansons de Geste*." Taine is charmed by this peace and simplicity: one would willingly remain in such company, he reflects, for primitive thought is wholesome thought. He is not sparing in his praise of the *Idylls*: he wonders at the purity and delicacy of figures such as Enid, at the grandeur of Arthur's death. Apparently, he notes, an archaeologist can re-create all styles except the grand style; but Tennyson has re-created everything, even the grand style. Nothing calmer or more imposing has been done since Goethe. This purity of style, this moral grandeur, are Tennyson's sole contributions to the poetry of his age. Lacking strong personal inspiration, he had to do over again, with finer and nobler art, what others had already done. His influence will be clearly marked only in the purity and loftiness of the moral emotion which people will gain from contact with Tennyson's work. But people will leave that work as they come out of a museum or picture-gallery. And the word *musée*, with its associations of culture, splendid art, and lifelessness, well conveys Taine's verdict on Tennyson. The next generation in France, as we shall see, made good use of the museum.

"We understand the flowers better when we see the garden." Thus Taine upheld his system, and as he worked out the case of Tennyson, the critic must have felt the pleasure of the mathematician who sees a perfect solution unfolding before him, or of the doctor when the disease corroborates the diagnosis. If ever a poet was the embodiment of his age and *milieu*, Tennyson was that poet, and the *milieu* that of well-to-do Englishmen under the glorious rule of Queen Victoria. He even embodied it to an extent that Taine never suspected, since Taine, as we have seen, judged such works as *Maud*, *The Princess*, and the *Idylls* entirely on their face value.

With delightful skill and more than a dash of malice, Taine describes England as he saw it. One seems to breathe the air of Harrow or Richmond. Everything is clean, neat, and deliciously green; even the modern houses with their gables and turrets have a Gothic look, smothered as they are in ivy, set among great trees and fresh lawns. The analogy is not hard to trace: it is of Tennyson's poetry that Taine is thinking when he exclaims, at the sight of this England: "How tidy and clean it is, how well everything is arranged, and kept up, and trimmed, to give comfort to the senses and pleasure to the eyes!" Then, in a passage which Brunetière considered to be one of the most heartfelt that he ever wrote,[1] Taine describes intellectual France concentrated in Paris, with its feverish pursuit of novelty, its artificial life full of strange and

[1] See *L'Évolution de la poésie lyrique*, vol. i. (Paris, 1894, p. 257).

abnormal sensations. Here young minds inherit doubt and scepticism as an Englishman inherits his principles and his faith. Yet here are heard the sublime cries of an Alfred de Musset, confessing all the sorrow of humanity from an *hôtel garni* in a sordid street. "We pity him, we think of that other poet who, over there in the Isle of Wight, is making a hobby of rewriting forgotten epics. How happy he is with his fine books, his friends, his honeysuckle and his roses. No matter. Our man, in this very place, in this mire and wretchedness, has risen to greater heights. With despair he has torn from his entrails the idea he had conceived, and has shown it to the eyes of all. That is more difficult and more splendid than fondling and contemplating the ideas of other men. There is only one work worthy of a man in this world: that is to bring forth a truth to which one gives one's whole self and in which one believes."

This is a striking contrast, and illustrates in an energetic way the characteristics of two very different poets. But when, having read this resounding conclusion, we lay down the book, and collect ourselves a little after being carried away by the rhythm of this reasoning, we wonder what it all proves. Taine considers that the poet of a rich, peaceful, moral England falls short of the poet of the hectic, artificial life of Paris. But even the calmest mothers have sometimes refractory children—this same peaceful and moral England gave birth to Shelley and Swinburne: and there is always Coppée (like Tennyson, popular and successful) to prove that one can be a true child of Paris without forthwith being gifted with a fine frenzy. While admitting the main truth of the argument as it stands, one feels that Taine is not quite playing the game. Or at least he is playing it on his own ground, by comparing the strength of the one to the weakness of the other. Tennyson is not Musset's English equivalent, and the comparison is in reality hollow. One might as well compare Keats with Hugo or Browning with Baudelaire.

M. André Chevrillon, recounting his recollections of Taine's old age, tells us how the critic, as his health failed, and all hope on his personal behalf vanished, came to love only those things which manifest life and health, and that true equilibrium and inward order from which creation gains unvarying strength and serenity. This attachment to life showed itself in his aesthetic judgments. More and more, in a work of art, he took into account what he called its characteristic degree of beneficent power. "If he had not loved Musset so much in his youth," concludes M. Chevrillon, "if he had read him for the first time about 1880 and compared him to Tennyson, I doubt whether his judgment would have been that of the *Littérature anglaise*, whether he would have preferred the sobs and the fevers of Rolla to the calm, lofty, and manly meditations of the English poet, to his pure and austere expressions of stoicism."[1]

This is only supposition, perhaps over-generous to Tennyson. But time did put Taine in the wrong. It is chiefly in Tennyson's work after 1860 that Taine's contradictors find their proof. Swinburne, for instance, in the characteristic article already quoted, affirms that four lines of *Rizpah* set in the balance would outweigh the most exquisite verse of Musset. But *Rizpah* was written in 1880.

One might with justice reproach Taine for giving no account, either in later editions of the *Littérature anglaise*

[1] *Revue de Paris*, June 1, 1908 (Taine: "Notes et Souvenirs," 3rd article, pp. 591, 592).

or in his *Notes sur l'Angleterre,* of Enoch Arden and the rustic poems published in 1864. But into the suave picture, the sort of *Embarquement pour Cythère* that Taine had made of Tennyson's poetry, he could hardly have introduced, even in the name of truth, the rough face of Enoch Arden or the Northern farmer. It would have upset the balance of the composition entirely.

Taine neglected nothing essential in Tennyson's work as it stood in 1860: one cannot maintain that he saw it whole.

II. *Montégut and Scherer*

Taine's brilliant work forestalled a series of studies which had long been maturing in the mind of an older critic, Emile Montégut, who, attracted by our literature, had spent a year in England (1852–1853) and was on terms of close friendship with certain English writers, notably Carlyle. Though thus well equipped for a study of contemporary English literature, Montégut did not want to deal with subjects already handled by Taine. In the case of Tennyson, who seems to be Montégut's favourite English poet, he fortunately made an exception. His first article, *Des premiers poèmes aux Idylles du Roi,* which appeared in the *Revue des Deux Mondes* of November 1850, long before the first studies of Taine, is followed up in 1866 by a second article, *Enoch Arden et les poèmes populaires.*[1] It seems as though Montégut were sorry to see Tennyson pigeon-holed by Taine: finding a new development in Tennyson, he wants to give him credit for it. Montégut is the fairest of critics, gifted with extraordinary sympathy and flexibility of thought. He is ready to modify

[1] R.D.M., March 1866.

his opinions: he has even the courage to admit his mistakes.

Montégut is not systematic. He realises that a critic's task is often one of sacrilege; he has too much respect for individuality to subordinate it to any theory; he is too conscious of the complexity of a poet's work to attempt to epitomise it in a few strokes. He seeks to reveal, by a series of impressions, all the delicate shades of a poetical work.

A critic much concerned with the moral significance of all art, Montégut grieves at the divorce of poetry from life which he sees becoming more and more marked. Old epic poetry reflects every aspect of human life; in Shakespeare's day poetry was still the expression of the thought of an age. Now the novel has replaced the epic; the only poetry which can survive is lyric poetry, giving expression only to the personality of the poet. This divorce is due less to the egoism of the poet than to the vulgar complexity of our daily life. To Montégut the life of his time is so prosaic, so stripped of all heroism—for our vices are as insignificant and bourgeois as our virtues—that the poet has to seek refuge in his own soul and treasure there the last vestiges of poetry. English poetry illustrates well this progressive detachment: reluctantly the poet withdraws himself from his kind. Wordsworth—a patient gleaner, Montégut calls him—is a touching example of a last compromise and proves the futility of the effort he makes. With Shelley the separation is complete: the poet lives in a world of illusion peopled by the visions of his own mind, and poetry becomes a dangerous narcotic, numbing us to reality. It is in this light that Tennyson's work first strikes Montégut. How willingly we forget with him the dullness and ignominy of real life, says

Montégut, identifying Tennyson with his Lotos-eaters; and again he declares, as if shaking off a spell, "I have drunk with delight at the spring of this poetry; the water which flows from it is cool, but somehow I think that the waters of Lethe must taste so. There is too much charm here, too much heady sweetness, too many invitations to dreaming and kindly sleep. Yes, poet, it is good to forget; but it is not healthy."

Montégut feels then all the beauty of Tennyson's verse, and finds to interpret that beauty images of peculiar aptness and charm, but he cannot help regretting in Tennyson a lukewarm attachment to those interests which are vital to humanity in general, and an indifference to higher truths which is that of a dilettante or a dandy. Like Taine, he considers that so far as poetry is concerned Tennyson has the soul of a dilettante, "and Fancy is his muse". He sees in the Lady of Shalott a symbol of the life of all artists, but above all of the life of Tennyson. Like her laid under a spell, he weaves a magic web before a mirror in which he sees only reflections of actual life; he is not privileged to mingle with the living. From this aloofness springs a certain cold elegance which is his most definite characteristic. Nature in Tennyson's poetry is *"lumineuse et sans chaleur"*; all his poems are fraught with *"cette froideur exquise, cette froideur brillante, cette clarté glacée"*. Even his emotion is cold and spiritualised; he purges emotions of all grossness, rejecting what is physical. Rarely does his elegant soul experience sentiments which are passionate, gloomy, poignant, or stormy.[1] Montégut points out that the sentiment of which he wrote with the greatest sincerity and depth of thought was the sentiment which is cold and complex beyond all others—friendship.

[1] Montégut excepts *Oenone, Fatima,* and *Maud.*

Having once levelled at Tennyson this reproach of coldness, Montégut gives high praise to *In Memoriam*. For him, the greatest merit of the poem is its accent of perfect sincerity. "We find here no poetical efforts on a large scale", the critic goes on, "no taxing of the imagination; the reader is ignored; the poet has uttered his lament from day to day, without troubling whether the effect might be monotonous. It is not to the public that the poem is addressed, but to the dead man himself. It is really a conversation with an unseen soul, full of assurances of sympathy, of faithful promises, of reproaches, of curious questionings, interrupted now and then by an interval of silence, as though waiting for an answer which does not come."

By a series of impressions, Montégut tries to present to his readers the figure of the poet whom he considers to be unique in contemporary literature. His method, less rigid than Taine's, reveals the little characteristic details, along with the less obvious aspects of the poet's talent. He finds in Tennyson, for example, an aptitude for expressing grace of movement: the transient elusive beauty of a pose, the lift of the head; an originality which Baudelaire carried further. He picks out also, and exaggerates, two decadent tendencies in Tennyson. The poet, lymphatic and nervous in temperament, is master of all the rhythms and cadences which make the nerves tingle and give a morbid kind of pleasure. He is decadent also in his love of Nature sickly and on the wane, as in autumn and early winter. Montégut seems to be the first French critic to point out the symbolic aspect of Tennyson's poetry. Thus to Montégut the Lotos-eaters may stand for all those who have given up struggling with life and have abandoned themselves to ease and forgetfulness. In the same way, through such symbols as Ulysses, Tithonus, and Arthur, Tennyson expresses most deeply the torment and sorrow of modern existence.

Enoch Arden reveals a Tennyson who, to a certain extent, belies Montégut's first judgment of him: the critic takes up his pen to sketch another impression of the poet. Montégut had already touched on the *douceur discrète* of the *Idylls*: now, when he thinks of Tennyson, the first words which come into his mind are *"la tranquillité, la fierté paisible."* Everything about him is serene, says Montégut: Tennyson's fame, as assured as any fame can be, is yet discreet, like his talent. The poet, by his restrained emotion, by the elegant melancholy of his voice, inspires not enthusiasm but sympathy. "His images are above all those which shed calm and quietude, even in the utterance of distress and grief; always, whether in joy or sorrow, he creates so deep a peace that my one care is not to use unwittingly some jarring word, some epithet which may make too much sound."

Enoch Arden marks for Montégut a change in Tennyson's attitude. He had always shown an interest in humble rustic life, giving, as in *The Miller's Daughter*, an idyllic glamour to reality. Montégut considers that this latest volume has almost a democratic flavour: the poet appears as a man talking to his brothers about his brothers; he looks reality full in the face. Montégut translates the whole of the poem *The Grandmother*, admiring it as a most complete and profound study of old age; he appreciates the humour of *The Northern Farmer*. Above all he admires the sober simplicity of the style in *Enoch Arden*, a style where neutral tones predominate, as in the countryside where the action takes place.

Montégut refrains from giving a final judgment on Tennyson; he would not have him other than he is, and is confident that whatever type of poem may attract him, Tennyson will not go wrong, being "so sure and so temperate in his tastes".

"The essence of poetry", writes Edmond Scherer in an essay on *L'Avenir de la poésie* (1868),[1] "is the imagination which takes delight in the visible, picturesque beauty of things and which renders that beauty by words which in their turn create an image." Poetry thus conceived has a language of its own, and Scherer gives as examples of this language first an image of Horace, and then a line of Shakespeare:

        And jocund day
Stands tiptoe on the misty mountain tops. . . .

To this "delightful, inimitable line, the finest imaginative line ever written", he pays Tennyson the high compliment of adding:

  Now lies the earth all Danaë to the stars.

Like Montégut, Scherer regrets that poetry is withdrawing more and more from the stream of modern life, and that the finest poetry, if it were to appear now, would make no stir in the world. "A few people of taste, a few men of letters, themselves the product of an artificial and obsolete culture, might read it. The public would remain indifferent."

It is as a phenomenon, then, that Scherer points out in the *Temps* of January 11, 1870, the great success of the *Holy Grail*. What a happy race are the English! he reflects. And what a fortunate writer is Tennyson! A new poem by

---

[1] *Études sur la littérature contemporaine*, vol. iv., 1873.

him is announced and immediately curiosity is aroused, and there is almost a public sensation. Scherer admires Tennyson's ability to keep up his intellectual standards, and his fidelity to his poetic vocation: he notes in him a love of perfection, and that "religion of work without which there results only sterile improvisation".

Here is the last of this series of idylls which, slowly evolved, "falls into our hands like a ripe and mellow autumn fruit". Tennyson has achieved the only epic possible in our days; he has imitated no one; he has ignored the classic recipes; he has kept the legendary fragrance of this tale of chivalry despite its modern point of view and its personal feeling. In this he differs from Goethe. Both of them, born in a period of science and reflection, found satisfaction in a superior, a sublime sort of pastiche. But whilst Goethe is careful to revive the spirit of a bygone age, Tennyson merely borrows the theme, to which he brings all his modern sentiments. "His King Arthur is noble, full of lofty and chivalrous morality, but, *juste ciel!* how far we are, in Tennyson, from the primitive stories which were the undoing of Francesca, from the ingenuous loves of Yseult or Guinevere".

Here lies the originality of a poet who does not invent his subjects. Scherer credits him with a remarkable faculty of analysing a psychological situation. Having found his theme, he dissects it, he scrutinises it, he treats it in a series of variations, and in the end throws into extraordinary relief the picture he paints, gives poignant intensity to the emotion he sings. Such is his method in *Ulysses*, the *Lotos-eaters*, and *Mariana*, the last, according to Scherer, possessing a weird power that is found in no other poem in the English language. This originality of Tennyson's was apparent even in the first volume of poems, amidst all the caprices of an airy, brilliant, and fantastic imagination: it was confirmed by the early Idylls as that of a simple, but strong and splendid genius. This second volume saved Tennyson from being considered—as for long enough was Alfred de Musset in France—solely as a writer of youthful fantasies. Instead of judging everything in the light of these early poems, Scherer sees in *The Princess*, *In Memoriam*, and the *Idylls* works excellent in their diversity, each having its own originality. (He has not a high opinion of *Maud*—"an obscure and sullen sort of rhapsody".) *The Princess* is one of the most charming and original of Tennyson's works: "it is high-spirited, it is out of the way, it is amusing, wise, and ridiculous in turn; it is the most delightful of extravaganzas". *In Memoriam* makes the deepest impression on the critic; the poem attracted by its boldness at a time when religious problems were not attacked in so direct a fashion in England.

Scherer defends Tennyson against those who compare him, as a thinker, unfavourably with Browning. He suggests that poetry can hold in solution, as it were, only a given quantity, and probably only a given quality, of philosophy.

Scherer sees all the beauty of Tennyson's work, but finds a grave fault at the heart of it. He gives him credit for its astonishing variety, and for all his skill. He agrees that certain of his lyrics are without equal in any language. He lacked one thing only, that supreme gift, that powerful beat of the wings which could bear Ganymede up to the empyrean and cast him quivering at the feet of Jupiter. His elegance itself becomes a fault: he is over-civilised, over-accomplished. Full of resource, Tennyson attempted all styles and all *genres*. He succeeded brilliantly in every one, yet no one can say that he plumbed anything to its depths. "There is a heat of passion, a tumult of the mind, a ruin of life's ideals, that Tennyson's verse is powerless to express. His poetry, whether deliberately or by reason of his inspiration I know not, keeps itself too strictly within the realm of what is seemly and conventional."[1]

With the vigorous and independent criticism of Scherer ends the judgment of the major critics on Tennyson. Those who read the studies of Taine, Montégut, and Scherer had, no doubt, a knowledge of all that Tennyson had written, and a very fair idea of his talent. They would be little disposed to seek any real feeling which lay hidden beneath a reserve which seemed mere coldness, beneath an elegance of form due to his artistic scruples. If he was judged with sympathy, it was of a detached and disinterested kind. Among the next generation of critics, less eminent, it is true, we find an important change of attitude.

[1] In Scherer's article on *Wordsworth et la poésie anglaise*, Tennyson is again discussed (*Études*, vol. vii.). A chapter on *Tennyson and Gladstone* appears in the *Études*, vol. x.

CHAPTER III

GROWTH OF TENNYSON'S REPUTATION—ADAPTATIONS AND TRANSLATIONS, 1850–1875

IN 1856 Lamartine, making a survey of European literature, seeks to rout any accusation of decadence. Naturally, in dealing with English literature, he goes back to Scott and Byron: more recently, the novels of Dickens and Thackeray, the essays of Macaulay, prove that the sap is still rising. Of poetry he makes no mention. At this time Tennyson had been Poet Laureate for six years.[1]

In France knowledge of Tennyson's work did not spread in any even way. Let us glance first at the periodicals interested in European literature. The *Revue britannique* continues to comment on Tennyson's poems and even goes so far as to reproach him for his silences.[2] The *Revue française*, founded in 1855, which was so receptive to foreign influence and whose contributors—Auguste Lacaussade for example—imitate or translate Keats, Burns, Cowper, and Wordsworth, never mentions Tennyson's name once in all its four years of life.

Similarly the *Bibliothèque universelle*, which is very much interested in Anglo-Saxon literature, and which in 1855 devotes two articles to Longfellow, has not much to say of Tennyson. In 1858 this review comments on the Pre-

---

[1] See *Cours familier de littérature*, vol. ii. pp. 20, 21, 1856.
[2] Nov. 1852, pp. 229-231, Dec. 1854, p. 491.

Raphaelite edition of his poem—"a fine volume worthy of the great poet" ... whose name is spelt Tennysson (January 1858, p. 120). In 1859 the *Bibliothèque universelle*, contrasting the simplicity of *Adam Bede* with the affectation prevalent in English literature—"*on nage en plein charlatanisme*"—condemns Tennyson's "subtle obscurities" with the rest. It is only in 1860, after the publication of the *Idylls of the King*, that we find an enthusiastic article on these "five pearls set in one ring": in these, we are told, Tennyson has proved himself the first of English poets, is indeed comparable to Shakespeare. Was there ever anything so fresh, so sweet, so chaste as the poem *Elaine*? and a long article gives a translation of practically the whole poem, interspersed with approving comments.[1]

The *Revue européenne* (1859) alludes more or less ironically to Tennyson's work.[2] In January 1860 its London correspondent announces that the great poet "who has so long rested on his oars, seems to have wakened up suddenly". This awakening gives no satisfaction to L. Étienne, who in the same review scathingly compares the virile efforts of Elizabeth Barrett Browning in *Poems before Congress* to the fair dreams and sweet harmonies of Tennyson. "The Poet Laureate, the athletic poet, *l'homme à la riche nature*, sings of King Arthur and Queen Guinevere, or lingeringly puts green English landscape into the most musical verse that the English language has known. It is like Hercules trying to be graceful and playing at knucklebones."[3] Another writer in the same review indignantly rejects any possible comparison between Tennyson and Hugo, between the audacities of the *Légende des Siècles*,

[1] *Bibliothèque universelle*, Sept. 1860, *Un poème de Tennyson*, by J. L. M.
[2] April 1859, p. 5; June 1859, p. 6.
[3] *Revue européenne*, Aug. 1860: *Les poètes anglais contemporains: leurs sentiments sur l'Empereur et sur l'Angleterre*.

and the placid susurration of the English bard.[1] Having delivered these observations, the *Revue européenne* relapses into silence on the subject of Tennyson. Gustave Masson in the *Correspondance littéraire* of September 5, 1859, reviews the Idylls of "*ce gentleman*", considers the poems quite noteworthy, but regrets that the Poet Laureate has not seen fit to clothe his thought in a garb more severe and more grandiose. The *Revue britannique* is led astray by the word Idylls, but boldly points out the originality of Tennyson's style and prophesies great popularity.[2]

Opinions on Tennyson's reputation abroad do not agree. In 1862 a correspondent of the *Revue britannique* doubts whether Tennyson is known in France in spite of the *Revue britannique*, "which has published in verse and prose divers samples of the work of the official successor of Southey and Wordsworth" (May, *Correspondance de Londres*). On the other hand, the *Bibliothèque universelle* (April 1865) prefaces its translation of an article of the *Quarterly Review* with the assurance that Tennyson is known throughout Europe.

However that may be, we can already find traces of an intimate knowledge of Tennyson's work. He has admirers, even imitators. Hippolyte Lucas is attracted by *Mariana* and *In Memoriam*, and attempts a translation of the former and of *Ring out, wild bells*. The choice is a natural but incautious one, because of the characteristic music of the English. These translations he sends to Tennyson, who points out what a poor language French is for translating English poetry. The rendering "*Sonnez, cloches, sonnez*", for "Ring out, wild bells", strikes him as absurd. The refrain of *Mariana*, "He cometh not, she said", is translated by

---

[1] *Revue européenne*, Sept. 1860, p. 176.
[2] *Rev. britannique*, July 1859, pp. 237-240.

GROWTH OF TENNYSON'S REPUTATION 45

Lucas "*Tom ne vient pas*". . . . In spite of this, Tennyson writes to thank Lucas for his friendly gesture, and even goes so far as to say that he is flattered by the resemblance to his own poem.[1]

André Theuriet has reason to be grateful to Tennyson when he makes his poetical debut in the *Revue des Deux Mondes* (August 1857). His poem *In Memoriam* is written to a Frenchwoman, who after a long stay in England infected him with her admiration of the English poets. Young Theuriet is jubilant at having his work accepted by so important and so exclusive a review: he puts it down to *"une sincérité émue et une fraîcheur d'impression qui donnaient à l'œuvre une sorte de beauté du diable"*. Tennyson had his share in this dewy freshness, for Theuriet inserts in his poem an adaptation of *Mariana*. His heroine is called Aimée: she is in exile in Germany: Mariana's poplar is disguised as a pine tree, but Aimée's plaint has a familiar ring:

> Quand sur le toit moussu glissait l'ombre du soir,
> Seule et se complaisant dans son âpre souffrance,
> Les yeux toujours tournés vers l'étendue immense,
> A sa fenêtre elle venait s'asseoir . . .
> Le vent faisait craquer la maison isolée.
> O Dieu, Dieu de merci, murmurait l'exilée,
> Je suis lasse, bien lasse et je voudrais mourir!
>
> Ce noir logis semblait hanté de mauvais rêves.
> Les portes sur leurs gonds criaient; dans la grand' salle
> Elle entendit des pas retentir sur la dalle
> Et des voix d'autrefois l'appelaient au dehors.

[1] See the letter quoted in the *Memoir*, vol. i. p. 385. Léo Lucas in *Les Correspondants d'Hippolyte Lucas* (in typescript at the Bibliothèque Nationale) also quotes it. The versions given by these two devoted sons are not identical. In that of Léo Lucas mention is made of a "lutte généreuse" in which Hippolyte Lucas championed Tennyson against the *Quarterly Review*, of which I have been able to find no details.

[2] See Theuriet's *Années de printemps*—a diary, p. 180.

> (All day within the dreamy house,
> The doors upon their hinges creaked. . . .
> Old footsteps trod the upper floors,
> Old voices called her from without. . . .)

A solitary pine grew close by:

> Quand la lune, à minuit, vers la vague calmée
> Descendait, le grand pin, près du chevet d'Aimée
> Dessinait son profil sur les pâles rideaux. . . .
> Éveillée en sursaut au bruit de la tempête,
> Prenez-moi, disait-elle, ô Dieu, me voilà prête.
> Je suis lasse, bien lasse, et je voudrais mourir.

> (But when the moon was very low,
> And the wild winds bound within their cell,
> The shadow of the poplar fell
> Upon her bed, across her brow, etc.).

Just as Theuriet finds in *Mariana* the most touching expression of a hopeless love, Félix Frank, a disciple of Theuriet, in *Le Poème de la Jeunesse*, seems to feel with the disillusioned lover of *Locksley Hall*, whose upbraidings he translates in a poem called *Ma Cousine Amy*. This cheapens or omits many images of the original poem:

> Elle se tourna, sous les bonds
> D'un flot de soupirs palpitante:
> Toute l'âme, *aurore éclatante*
> Parut dans ses yeux noirs profonds.

> (And she turned—her bosom shaken with a sudden storm of sighs,
> All the spirit deeply dawning in the dark of hazel eyes.)

> Aux doux bruits du taillis voisin
> Bien des matins sur la bruyère
> Par son *haleine printanière*
> J'ai senti *se gonfler mon sein*.

(Many a morning on the moorland did we hear the
 copses ring,
And her whisper thronged my pulses with the full-
 ness of the spring.)

Ah, *quels transports*
Ont joint nos cœurs d'un baiser chaste!

(And our spirits rushed together at the touching of
 the lips.)

In 1859 we find a diverting adaptation of a poem of Tennyson's. Jules Tardieu, the publisher, on a visit to an English friend at Boulogne-sur-mer, takes a fancy to Tennyson's poetry and publishes, under the pseudonym of J. T. de Saint-Germain, a rendering in prose of *Lady Clare*. His book bears as epigraph a line of *In Memoriam*—"Ring in the love of truth and right"—and the author, in telling the story of the faithful lovers, cannot help moralising a little, contrasting this fine disinterestedness with the widespread system of *"mariages d'intérêt"*. Each chapter bears at its head a verse of *Lady Clare*: it takes two hundred and twenty pages to tell the story that Tennyson tells in twenty-two verses, but in justice to M. J. T. de Saint-Germain it must be admitted that he did his best to improve it. Lady Clare is the heiress of the Douglases and lives in Cumnor Castle on the banks of the Clyde. Her russet gown becomes a coarse red dress under a plaid cloak. There is a villain, a saucy page-boy, a maiden aunt. The heroine falls ill and there is a melodramatic dénouement—the wronged heiress is recognised by the mark of a fleur-de-lys which she bears, poetically, *"à l'endroit où bat son cœur."*

But these are only isolated cases. Of more importance is the essay in rural poetry in the style of

Tennyson's English idylls, made about this time by Joseph Autran.

This brings us in touch with a large subject. In French rural poetry there are several currents which meet and mingle. Along with the rural epic in the Lamartinian tradition, we find the little homely poem of country life which approaches the *roman en vers*. A third current shows itself in the forest poetry of Theuriet and his imitators. We shall see that Tennyson's influence was only felt in the familiar type of poetry, though he was known to the forest poets.

Tennyson, of course, had no monopoly of this genre in English poetry, but Autran evidently takes Tennyson as his master since *La Vie rurale* (1856), a series of poems in the manner of the English idylls, includes an adaptation of *Dora*. Autran in his preface maintains that in country life lies the only fresh source of poetry nowadays, and prides himself on being among the first in France to seek new inspiration there. The notion was not as novel as Autran thought it. Lamartine's *Jocelyn* had set the example, as well as Brizeux' *Marie*. But Autran, like Tennyson, does not attempt the epic style. The poems are merely episodes, the interest is focussed on two or three persons only. They are less diffuse, less sentimental than *Jocelyn*: they give a more real or perhaps more realistic portrayal of country life, with a realism that entails no ugliness, but tells of ordinary life in all its simplicity—the realism of George Eliot, for example. Tennyson, in his English idylls, has not yet attained the simplicity and sobriety of *Enoch Arden:* he idealises his characters, poses them becomingly, as in the *Gardener's Daughter*; but even then he falls far short of such pretentious, not to say operatic, effects as the awakening of the village maidens in the first pages of *Jocelyn*.[1] It is Laprade who, in *Pernette*, carries on the tradition of Lamartine and the rural epic. Autran, with much less talent and much less taste than Laprade, has a claim to our interest in that he attempted to popularise in his own tongue the short familiar poem of Tennyson.

La Vie rurale, then, contains an adaptation, or rather a translation, of *Dora* under the title *Gertrude* (*d'après* Tennyson). Autran tells this simple story as Tennyson tells it, concisely, without any elaboration, and sets beside it original poems of the same order: *La Fille du Meunier*—the title is again reminiscent of Tennyson—an incident which comes to disturb the peace of a village; *Victoire Aubier*, the sad and improbable tale of a farmer's son who casts out his own mother, ruins his father, and takes his own life; *Blanche de Reillane*, an idyll of the *vie de château*, wherein a frivolous old uncle is converted by a pious niece. Autran's touch is less sure than that of Tennyson, who for the most part is content with the most ordinary occurrences of life, building up his tales round feelings and failings common to us all—the obstinacy of the old farmer in *Dora*, the loquacity of the miller in *The Brook*—whereas Autran's effects tend to be more melodramatic.

Laprade, who with Autran forms a little meridional brotherhood of rural poets, has no use for Tennyson: he knows his work superficially and despises it. He considers that *Jocelyn* is infinitely superior to anything achieved in

[1] "Les filles du village, à ce refrain joyeux,
Entr'ouvraient leur fenêtre en se frottant les yeux,
Se saluaient de loin de sourire ou de geste,
Et sur les hauts balcons penchant leur front modeste,
Peignaient leurs longs cheveux qui pendaient en dehors
Comme des écheveaux dont on lisse les bords;
Puis elles descendaient nu-pieds, demi-vêtues
De ces plis transparents qui collent aux statues
Et cueillaient sur la haie ou dans l'étroit jardin
L'œillet ou le lilas tout baignés du matin...."

E

this style either in England or Germany.[1] However, in his study, *Du sentiment de la Nature chez les modernes* (1868), Laprade devotes a whole section of his book to analysing the attitude of English poets to Nature, and since Tennyson is the only contemporary poet mentioned, Laprade must allow him a certain importance. He does not find much that is good to say of this 'Tennisson'. Laprade has certainly read Taine: it is less certain that he has read Tennyson. Crushing sarcasm flows from his pen, but in the whole article he does not mention a single poem of Tennyson's.

What a deplorable contrast, says Laprade, between the great Alpine wastes evoked by the poetry of Byron, "that great outlaw of thought", and "the well-tilled slopes around London, the parks and cottages of happy and good-living families", where the chaste muse of the Poet Laureate loves to roam. Laprade has a very quaint idea of Tennyson as a Nature poet. "With Tennisson the representation of the outside world resembles too often the landscape of a botanical garden or a hothouse. Exotic flowers, oriental colours and odours abound, tastefully blended and grouped with the shrubs of our own clime, as in the vases of a wealthy drawing-room.[2] The charm of these amiable compositions cannot be denied. One revels in them on a comfortable sofa. But by living in this balmy atmosphere where the wind does not blow enough, one feels smitten with a sort of moral headache." I reproduce no more; the whole article is worth reading. Laprade passes by the "judicious Tennisson" in order to

---

[1] See in *Essais de critique idéaliste* (Paris, 1882), the essay on Lamartine.
[2] This is Taine: "Sa poésie ressemble à quelqu'une de ces jardinières dorées et peintes où les fleurs nationales et les plantes exotiques emmêlent dans une harmonie savante leurs torsades et leurs chevelures " (vol. iv. p. 475).

worry himself about the future of the poetry of Nature, menaced by the danger of exoticism.

Besides these adaptations of Tennyson, we find several attempts at translation, which aim at making the poet's work familiar in France.

This brings us to the knotty old problem of the value of translations in verse—an insoluble problem, since so much depends on the talent and tact of the translator. Generally speaking, Tennyson does not lend himself to verse translation. He once said, using the French words, that lines of verse ought to be *beaux comme de la prose*, having the same dignity, the same freedom, the same suppleness of rhythm. Tennyson's most exquisite songs dispense with rhyme— *Tears, idle tears*, for instance. Thus Tennyson's verse can be but poorly represented in Alexandrines, where the rhyme recurs with relentless emphasis.[1] In any but skilled hands the use of the Alexandrine entails much padding, many forced and banal rhymes which sound like metronome taps in the flow of the full, fluid music. Besides, in French, as M. Lanson points out with reference to a translation of Tennyson, the metre has too familiar a ring—"how can one prevent this Alexandrine from ringing in our ears like a well-known tune, bringing in its very accent and cadence something of the French tradition?" Since all translation is a betrayal, translation into verse is a double betrayal, in M. Lanson's opinion.

[1] This difficulty has been recognised by Fernand Baldenne, who in *En Marge de la vie* (Paris, *La Plume*, 1901) gives an admirable version of this poem. The unrhymed fifth line goes some way towards imitating the effect of the original blank verse. The third stanza reads:
"Tristes étrangement, comme à l'aube incertaine
Le gazouillis d'oiseaux assoupis, que perçoit
L'oreille d'un mourant, tandis que son œil voit
Blêmir en blanc carré la fenêtre prochaine,
Tristes étrangement, les jours qui ne sont plus. . . ."

One cannot, however, take up too rigorous an attitude towards these translations—if they are sometimes a betrayal indeed, they have had as their starting-point a wish to honour the poet. We shall have the opportunity of comparing the success of prose and verse translations.

In 1862 a certain Chevalier de Châtelain, a Frenchman living in London, and sometime winner of the Dunmow Flitch, attempts a translation of *Beautés de la poésie anglaise*. His aim, according to his preface, is to familiarise the continental public with English poetry: he translates only because of the stringency of copyright.[1] The first poem of Tennyson's that he tackles is *The Brook*, a good choice, but one which has many snags for the translator, of which the inconsequent song of the brook itself is one:

> I chatter over stony ways,
>   In little sharps and trebles,
> I bubble into eddying bays,
>   I babble on the pebbles. ...

This difficulty, added to that of the rhyme, leads him into much padding and such absurdities as:

> J'arrive au galop chez Philippe
> Noyer mes eaux au fleuve que j'agrippe.

> (Till last by Philip's farm I flow
> To join the brimming river.)

or:

> ... et quelquefois prêt à mourir de peur
> Je porte sur mon dos un poisson, c'est licite.

> (And here and there a lusty trout
> And here and there a grayling).

[1] See the preface of the first volume of *Beautés de la poésie anglaise* (5 vols., London, 1862, *et sqq.*). Vol. ii. includes three poems by Tennyson: *The Brook*, *Mariana*, and *Love and Death*. Vol. v. gives an indifferent translation of *The Eagle*, and a further volume, *Rayons et Reflets* (London, 1863), includes a feeble echo of *In Memoriam*, cvi.

He often mangles a good image, and that not for brevity's sake. In simpler and more straightforward passages his translation has a certain vigour, some happy turns of expression. His rendering of *Mariana*, another very difficult poem, is much more successful: the epithets are well-chosen, and, with a few exceptions, the whole thing is done with more imagination. Elaine's little song, *Sweet is true love, tho' given in vain, in vain*, written almost entirely in monosyllables, necessarily becomes a little heavy in translation, nor has the translator seen fit to retain the repetition of the words 'sweet' and 'bitter' which give the song such perfect simplicity. Let it be said for the Chevalier de Châtelain, however, that his choice is representative: an English idyll, the finest of the early poems, one of Tennyson's characteristic songs, and a poem from *In Memoriam*.

A more dignified attempt is made by H. Gomont, who prudently restricts himself to prose. He writes in the *Revue de l'Est* of January 1865:[1] "Byron and Shelley are known in France, but not Tennyson, and I think that he has the right to be not only known, but enjoyed." Gomont, who is himself something of a classical poet, admires most of all in Tennyson the poems of classical inspiration—*The Lotos-Eaters, Oenone*: "In them reigns an Ionian suavity, the simple, natural, easy flow of antique thought, delicately tinged with modern sadness." He does not take *The Idylls of the King* seriously: he considers that they will have little success in France, being "mere badinage, fairy-tales striving after *naïveté*." On the other hand, he takes the philosophy of Tennyson very seriously, finds boldness and originality in *The Two Voices*, of which he gives an excel-

---

[1] This article and the accompanying translations were published in book form, Metz, 1865.

lent analysis fully illustrated by translations; and in *In Memoriam*, "where Tennyson made himself the interpreter of modern feeling with a boldness of thought and language which recall Pascal". Gomont gives an admirable translation of five poems from *In Memoriam*, to which he adds, to demonstrate Tennyson's versatility, *Claribel* and *The Goose*. He calls for a complete translation of Tennyson. "My object has only been", he writes, "to point out the the existence of a true poet to those interested in the progress of ideas in England, and to those who will be pleased at the prospect of a new source of pure and noble enjoyment."[1]

Throughout this period the *Revue britannique* continues its translations of Tennyson, wisely restricting them to prose versions. An anonymous translator of *The Brook* (May 1865) undertakes to pay a year's subscription of the *Revue* for anyone who will attempt a verse translation. His own prose translation keeps close to the original, yet is easy, and sacrifices none of the spontaneity of the English poem.

Tennyson's works appeared in the Tauchnitz edition from 1868 onwards. As soon as *The Holy Grail* appears, the *Revue britannique* announces that it is to be had in the Tauchnitz edition at Reinwald's in the rue des Saints-Pères (January 1870). Boasting that it was among the first to bring Tennyson to the public notice, the *Revue britannique* publishes in the same year (April 1870, p. 395) a prose translation of *Pelleas and Ettarre*—presumably by Amédée

[2] In Gomont's *Poésies nouvelles* (Paris, 1864) the poem *La Dame blanche de Bonnaut* is reminiscent, both in metre and in theme, of *The Lady of Shalott*. Of another poem, *Le Vieux Chêne*, Gomont says: "Tennyson, le poète-lauréat anglais, est l'auteur d'une pièce de vers intitulée *The Old Oak*. Elle ressemble un peu à la nôtre." Since Tennyson's poem (*The Talking Oak*) was written first, it might be more exact to say that his resembles Tennyson's.

Pichot. A bibliographical note is tacked on, inviting readers to compare the idyll in the Tauchnitz edition with Malory's tale in the edition of Thomas Wright. It is, in fact, more a translation of the story than of Tennyson's poem, explicit rather than poetical, omitting many of the images which lend colour to the poem, even omitting the little song *A rose, but one, no other rose had I.*

Xavier Marmier contributes two translations to the *Revue britannique*—*The May Queen*, a simple and adequate prose translation, marked off in verses, a method admirably suited to this poem full of naïve repetitions, with its monotonous refrain. In July 1877 appears a translation of *Enoch Arden* which we shall consider later.

A translation of *Lucretius* in the *Nouvelle Revue de Paris* offers a good example of the long-windedness which is too often the result of an attempt at a translation in verse.[1] The choice is original: a philosophic poem concise in style and apt in epithet. It takes 419 Alexandrines to render Tennyson's 280 lines: the translation has neither the incisiveness nor the energy of the original.

Let her that is the womb and tomb of all,	Puisse dans sa bonté la nature féconde,
Great Nature, take, and forcing far apart	Source et tombeau de tout ce qui passe en ce monde,
Those blind beginnings that have made me man,	Une seconde fois m'abriter dans son sein,
Dash them anew together at her will	Dissoudre de mon corps les débris insensibles,
Thro' all her cycles—into man once more,	Et les réunissant de sa puissante main
	Les lancer à travers ces cercles invisibles

[1] *Nouv. Revue de Paris*, Dec. 1868, p. 534, signed P. M.

Or beast or bird or fish, or opulent flower.	Pour en former encor peut-être un être humain Ou bien quelque animal, quelque fleur opulente, L'arbre aux fruits savoureux, l'abeille vigilante Ou l'oiseau dans les airs, le poisson dans les eaux.

None the less, credit is due to the translator for putting into French a poem which reveals a little-known side of Tennyson.

There is after all nothing better than rhythmical prose for translating Tennyson's verse, be it the supple and varied blank verse, or the lighter metres of his ballads. The most interesting translation of this period, Mallarmé's *Mariana*, is indeed a prose poem. Mallarmé was not lavish with his translations; they are his homage to the poet translated. His interpretation of Tennyson's poem comes even before his translations of Poe. It was in *La Dernière Mode*, that queer review founded by Mallarmé, in which he wrote everything, including the fashion notes, himself, that there appeared, under the title *Figurines d'Album*, this translation of *Mariana*, the sole contribution to this number (October 18, 1874), which openly bears Mallarmé's signature.

Mallarmé's choice is characteristic: one can well imagine that this poem fascinated him. As an expression of hopelessness and monotony it has never been bettered, even by Baudelaire, past master in the art of evoking dark moods. In its dream-like atmosphere, its wealth of detail, its complete absence of moral significance, it resembles much of the poetry that was being written in France towards the end of the century. Had the poet seen fit to suggest that Mariana represented his own soul or state of mind, the poem might well have served as a model to many a French symbolist poet of the nineties.

With perfect skill and sympathy Mallarmé keeps the desolate atmosphere of *Mariana*. Only once or twice does he fail to give the full value to Tennyson's imagery. The translation has in its simplicity a strange beauty, and leaves as clear an impression as the original poem:

> Les endroits à fleurs avaient une croûte épaisse de mousse très noire, tous de même. Les clous rouillés tombaient des attaches qui tinrent la pêche aux murs du jardin. Les appentis brisés, étranges et tristes; le bruyant loquet était sans se lever; sarclée et usée, l'ancienne paille sur la grange solitaire du fossé. Elle dit uniquement: "Ma vie est morne, il ne vient point", dit-elle; elle dit, "Je suis lasse, lasse, je voudrais être morte!"
>
> Et toujours, quand baissa la lune, et que les vents aigus se levèrent hauts et loin, dans le rideau blanc elle vit d'ici à là l'ombre secouée se balancer. Mais quand la lune fut très bas et les sauvages vents liés dans leur prison, l'ombre du peuplier tomba sur son lit, par-dessus son front. Elle dit uniquement: "La nuit est morne, il ne vient pas", dit-elle; elle dit: "Je suis lasse, lasse, je voudrais être morte!" . . .
>
> Le moineau pépiait sur le toit, le lent tic-tac de l'horloge et le bruit qu'au vent faisait le peuplier confondaient tous ses sens; mais le plus elle maudit l'heure où le rayon du soleil gisait au travers des chambres, quand le jour penchait vers le bosquet occidental. Alors elle dit, "Je suis morne, il ne viendra pas", dit-elle; elle pleura; "Je suis lasse, lasse ô Dieu!"

The *Revue indépendante* of February 1880 praises the translation as a charming poem from "the same subtle hands that put Poe into French. In it the hermit of the Isle of Wight is neither betrayed nor made insipid, as is generally the case."

These adaptations and translations of Tennyson's poems show an interest which overlooks no aspect of his art; he is here represented as a poet of country life and of legend, a poet who sees in the life of antiquity symbols of modern life, a philosophical poet, a humorous poet even, a poet distilling strange beauty. And as we go on, we find that with a better understanding comes a better interpretation.

CHAPTER IV

FORTUNE OF THE LONGER POEMS UNTIL 1892: TRANSLATIONS OF THE "IDYLLS OF THE KING", "ENOCH ARDEN", AND "MAUD"

FRANCE was the home of the traditional poetry to which Tennyson had recourse in *Idylls of the King*. In the land of their origin these legends had, since the Middle Ages, provided material for literary and historical research rather than themes for poetic treatment. Brizeux had planned an ambitious poem dealing with the heroic age of his native Brittany. According to notes left by him, *La Table Ronde ou la Chute de Bretagne* was to consist of a trio of narrations, containing about three thousand lines in all, with Arthur, Merlin, and Tristan as heroes. The project never took shape.[1] On the theme of Merlin, Edgar Quinet had written an allegorical novel, *Merlin l'Enchanteur* (1860): but this work, dealing largely in abstract ideas of a humanitarian kind, by no means sought to set the old legends in a new light. On the other hand several English poets, notably Milton and Southey, had been attracted by the Arthurian legends before Tennyson gave them new life in his own idylls and through his influence over poets like Morris.

[1] See in the *Œuvres complètes de Brizeux* (Michel Lévy, 1860), the foreword by Saint-René Taillandier, pp. lv, lvi, and also H. Finistère, *A. Brizeux et l'idée bretonne* (1888), p. 50. Brizeux alludes to it in his poems:
"Si la mort l'eût permis, Arthur, la Table Ronde
Eût été le pavois et le centre du monde".
Cf. *Les Bretons*, chap. xiii. p. 195.

H. de la Villemarqué, author of various studies on the Arthurian legend, notes, in the 1860 edition of *Romans de la Table Ronde*, the existence of the *Idylls* of 'Tennisson', and writes as though Southey were still the English Poet Laureate. . . .

Francisque Michel, an archaeologist and professor of foreign literature at the Faculté of Bordeaux, took a more definite interest in the *Idylls*, for it is to him that we owe the only complete French translation of the four idylls *Enid, Vivien, Elaine, Guinevere* which form the nucleus of the Tennysonian cycle.

The *Idylls*, with their blank verse, and their rich but sober language, lend themselves better to translation than any other poem except *Enoch Arden*. This translation appears in most agreeable form—an excellent prose rendering illustrated by engravings after Gustave Doré, who had already collaborated in an English edition of the *Idylls*. Published by Hachette, the four handsome folio volumes appeared, just about the Christmas season, in successive years: *Élaine* in 1867, *Viviane* and *Genièvre* in 1868, *Énide* in 1869. They were dedicated to Napoleon III. Later all four idylls were collected into one volume—*Les Idylles du Roi*.

Francisque Michel, in this translation, keeps very close to the original text without sacrificing dignity to accuracy. He renders Tennyson's verse with remarkable skill, transposing the slightest image without destroying its original grace. The strong natural style is so even that it is difficult to quote a particularly successful passage. The whole effect is successful.[1] But Doré's share in the production makes the greater impression on the reader's mind. Doré

---

[1] In translating *Merlin and Vivien*, Francisque Michel omits the long digression about Mark at the beginning.

seems to have appropriated a certain share of the glory due to Tennyson, and quite outshines the translator, who, having done his best, had naturally to efface himself in order that Tennyson might more clearly appear. Doré's illustrations had an interest of their own, and stood out from the text with a special effect.

Tennyson, although on good terms with *le bon Doré* (he lunched at the Moulin Rouge with him on his way through Paris in 1868), was not altogether pleased with his illustrations. We are not told why. Some displeasure, apart from an artist's jealousy for his own creations, was justified. Doré had little knowledge of English, and was unable to refer directly to Tennyson's poems. Thus, in spite of his powerful imagination, he did not quite enter into the Tennysonian atmosphere. The *Idylls*, which idealise ordinary life without losing contact with it, have a luminous, youthful quality, with which goes a good deal of gaiety and movement. In these four idylls, of course, we no longer find that candid happiness of the first days, when the May sun shone in Camelot upon the cloth of gold spread for the marriage of Arthur. Yet even in *Enid* and the other poems there are cheerful glimpses which make more impressive the gathering gloom. We remember Arthur's hunting in *Enid*, or the bustle of preparation on the eve of a tourney in the little town where Enid lived, or the splendour of the royal tournaments where Arthur sat in his robe of scarlet samite patterned with golden dragons. None of this gaiety enters into the sombre and fantastic visions of Doré. Only rarely does he portray some moment of vague tenderness—as in his conception of Enid and her mother going down the meadows at dawn, or Lancelot and Guinevere riding towards Camelot on a bright spring morning. In general the artist has let his imagination play over scenes of violence and mystery —stormy skies, deadly combats in dark forests, castles perched high on precipitous rocks, uprooted trees, and desolate pools. Doré, who always worked with enthusiasm, took such a keen interest in the *Idylls* that he wished to collaborate at an opera on the theme of Vivien.[1] Jules Claretie is of opinion that the illustrations to the *Idylls* are among the artist's best work. "His fantasy, his imagination were at their ease in this dream world. With powerful poetic vision, he evoked the deep glades of Druidic oaks in the dark forest of Broceliande."[2] Such are indeed the aspects which most attracted him and which he best interpreted.

He is less happy in his interior scenes, which have a chilly air of unreality, and lack both the rudeness required by historical accuracy and the legendary glamour which Tennyson cast over them. They are over-civilised, with their stained glass and sculptured cloister-walks. In the scenes at Almesbury, whereas Tennyson shows us Guinevere listening sadly in the light of a solitary candle to the innocent singing of the novice, Doré depicts Guinevere wild with grief, apostrophising the stars from the top of a flowery terrace that would better have suited Juliet or Jessica.

Nevertheless Doré's drawings have a character of their own, and their effect is vivid and lasting. One does not forget Elaine, drifting down to Camelot, a lily in her hands, with the mists of a summer morning about her. The whole atmosphere is suffused with exquisite tenderness and melancholy. One does not forget the desolate

[1] With Charles-Marie Widor. Nothing ever came of it. See *The Life of G. Doré*, by Blanche Roosevelt (London, Sampson & Low), 1885, p. 311.
[2] J. Claretie, *Peintres et sculpteurs contemporains* v. *G. Doré*, Paris, 1883, p. 118.

FORTUNE OF THE LONGER POEMS   63

heath where Arthur finds the skeletons of the two brothers who fought to the death, one skull still wearing the crown of diamonds; nor Vivien flying in the storm leaving behind her Merlin asleep for ever in Broceliande; nor the child Arthur found by Merlin on a dark shore lashed by an angry sea.

It had already been said of the Moxon edition to which Doré contributed that "it gave wings to Mr. Tennyson's muse. . . . These wings bore the idylls into foreign lands and gave them new life."[1] French critics certainly considered that the value of this translation of the *Idylls* was due to Doré's collaboration. "The engravings are just what is needed; they hold the attention, and suggest the poet's thought without revealing too much, so that one would wish to read the work, even were it not signed Alfred Tennyson", writes a critic of the *Revue de l'Instruction publique* on the subject of *Élaine*. Only after this compliment does the critic observe that Tennyson, "as a poet of tender and delicate emotions, seems to have surpassed himself in the graceful poem *Élaine*", and offer his thanks to Francisque Michel for having disclosed in his translation the poet's own words and the poet's very soul. Another critic of the same *revue* doubts whether Michel, with all his skill, will succeed in making Tennyson popular in France; he speaks of the impossibility of rendering into French this curious complex style, and considers that Doré's illustrations will do more than any translation to enhance Tennyson's reputation with the public and even among men of letters.[2] The *Constitutionnel* is more decided still—"The pencil of an artist to whom nothing is im-

---

[1] See the life of Doré by his English friend Blanchard Jerrold: *The Life of Gustave Doré* (London, W. H. Allen, 1891), p. 145.
[2] *Revue de l'Instruction publique*, Dec. 31, 1868, p. 646.

possible has translated, and with success, that which M. Taine did not dare to translate. All the delicacy, the grace and the charm of the English poet are admirably conveyed by this Proteus of the pencil" (December 31, 1868). One of these notices does not even mention the translator's name.[1]

It is curious to note the general attitude towards the *Idylls* themselves. Critics agree upon their beauty and charm—"they are real jewels, mounted with exquisite art.... We are still under the spell of this grace, elegance and purity."[2] It is through this translation, they affirm, that Tennyson has become known. Until recently, says a writer in the *Revue de l'Instruction publique*, little was known of Tennyson in France except his name noticed by chance on the title-page of a volume at some English bookseller's, or brought to one's notice in the pages of a review (December 31, 1868). They are interested in Tennyson's handling of these old legends. They note to what extent he has adapted and changed them — how, for example, the Vivien of the old stories was a mischievous fairy, whilst in Tennyson she is cunning and treacherous, not loving Merlin, but the power which the magic spells give her. "Although the phrase 'old fool!' at the end reveals to us the ironical intention of the poem", writes A. Blot in the *Revue de l'Instruction publique* (December 24, 1868), "I ask leave of M. Villemarqué not to call curses on the English author, but to admire at my ease the grace, the fantasy, and the sparkling wit of this charming work." Similarly it is seen that in *Enid* Tennyson keeps the bare

[1] *Ibid.*, Dec. 30, 1869, E. Montigny on *Énide*. Later critics are not always so enthusiastic about Doré: see the *Bibliothèque universelle* for April 1888, p. 107.
[2] From *Le Constitutionnel* (see above), which cannot resist using the consequences of Guinevere's sin to point a moral.

facts whilst altering the general plan of the legend which becomes, as it were, his own property, "by the invention of curious details, by a profound study of the characters, by a more delicate touch, sentimentally, and above all by the way in which the gentle, melancholy figure of Enid is brought into relief" (*ibid.*, December 30, 1869). Utterly forgotten since the days of Chrestien de Troyes, the legend, thanks to Tennyson, reappears "younger and more brilliant than ever. . . . And here this simple girl from the green Devonshire meadows comes to us, to mingle with the heroes of our own days: she brings into our cramped *salons*, into our stuffy atmosphere, the strong living fragrance of the forests."

The word *salons* gives us pause. We think of this costly edition which the *Mouvement littéraire* refers to as being intended above all for "lovers of beautiful books, connoisseurs in *éditions de luxe*, collectors of engravings by masters" (December 11, 1869). The words 'keepsakes' and 'guéridons', constantly recurring in the press notices, suggest an exquisite volume, made to be fingered absentmindedly in odd moments. A saying of Mallarmé's about "*cette édition d'in-folio luxueux close sur une version des Idylles*" comes to mind. But that was not quite the case.[1] In 1873 a critic of the *Journal des Débats* regretted that the French poets had left to an Englishman the glory of reviving the old Breton legends. "We wish the English Poet Laureate might find some imitators in this country. Why should

---

[1] Messrs. Hachette have been kind enough to supply details of these publications:
Élaine, 2 editions—500 in 1867, 1700 in 1868.
Énide, 2175 in 1869.
Geniève, 2200 in 1868.
Viviane, 2200 in 1868.
Of *Les Idylles du Roi* (the four *Idylls* in one volume) only 100 copies were printed. These volumes had a steady, if not a rapid, sale.

F

not Arthur, Guinevere, Lancelot, and Tristan live again in the language in which formerly they shone with such splendour?"[1] These legends never inspired a work of any length, but in certain circles they were to excite admiration devout enough to be called a cult: Tennyson, we shall see, had something to do with that movement.

In England *Enoch Arden* had a tremendous and immediate success among a public prepared to admire without criticism a poem from the Laureate. As a critic of the *Times* remarked, the point was reached where Tennyson was Tennyson, just as Allah was Allah, and there was nothing more to be said. Certain critics were hostile; but they showed better appreciation of their public than of the poem by attacking it not on artistic but on moral grounds. They objected that in this affair of unconscious bigamy the culprit is made to keep our sympathy, and that therefore the more poetic the representation the more immoral the poem. The *Times* reproaches Tennyson with having created poetic effects from a situation which Christian literature would do better to pass over in silence. The critic of the *Athenaeum* is even more emphatic in his protests against this 'prostitution of art': "Do we wish the young women of this generation to believe", he asks, "that it is a poetical incident rather than a dark and shameful misfortune to have two husbands alive at the same time? An agreeable impression!" The whole poem is a 'contribution to the sum of human weakness' (August 13, 1864).

Such scruples in no way trouble the French critics, who are inclined to smile at the susceptibility of their

---

[1] *Journal des Débats*, Feb. 2, 1873, in a review of *Les Romans de la Table Ronde*, by Paulin Paris.

English colleagues. They are ready to uphold the point of view of this new and less immaculate Tennyson. The *Revue britannique* contends that, though the subject may appear vulgar, the poem displays all the better the genius of Tennyson, who has succeeded in ennobling it by the loftiness of style and sentiment (September 1864). An early article in the *Revue de Paris* takes its information from the *Times*, but arrives at a totally different conclusion, namely, that Tennyson, in entering on this new path, may find some stumbling-block to that incomparable reputation that he enjoys among his fellow-countrymen. Yet this may also be the starting-point of a happy transformation. By reason of this wider, more human inspiration, he may be enabled to take rank among the universal geniuses, instead of finding his influence confined to England.[1]

Armand Renaud, in the *Revue contemporaine* (January 1866) likewise defends Tennyson against the ridiculous charges of immorality brought against him by "*le cant britannique*". He maintains that in *Enoch Arden* all the interest centres in the characters, especially that of Enoch. Now in the characters there is no moral flaw. The immorality, if it exists, must be in the situation, which Tennyson keeps in the background. Renaud reminds puritanical critics that "*il faut frapper peu pour frapper fort*". He also sees in the author of *Enoch Arden* a more human Tennyson. "This story, contrary to what the talent of Tennyson had led one to expect, touches the heart, brings tears to the eyes, moves us this time. Both the form and the matter have felt the influence of this transformation in him: the style keeps close to reality, and as Tennyson has not for that reason ceased to be a master of harmony, his realism is in the highest degree poetical."

[1] *Revue de Paris*, nouv. série, Sept. 1864, p. 586.

The poem belied many ideas about Tennyson which had hitherto held good in France, and was all the more important for that reason. Its faults, which corresponded to essential weaknesses of Tennyson's genius, escaped notice. The lifelessness of the characters, the entire lack of dramatic interest, and the stiff, humourless handling of the theme, were blemishes quite overshone by the glamour of his name. Moreover, the poem was accessible and translatable. One of the poet's aims had been to achieve a fine simplicity of style, in contrast to the elusive, highly wrought earlier manner. There was also the interest of the pathetic little story itself. It is no wonder, then, that between the year of its publication and Tennyson's death, *Enoch Arden* was translated at least eight times.

The first translation, appearing in 1868,[1] was by that P. M. whose *Lucretius* has already been noted. This time he contented himself with prose, so that the movement of the story is more rapid. His translation is accurate, and of some interest in itself, but the effect of the prose is quite different from that of the original blank verse. A short quotation shows its qualities and defects. Annie, overcome by her misfortunes, is thanking Philip for his offer to send the children to school.

"I came to speak to you of what he wished, Enoch, your husband. . . ."	"Je suis venu pour vous entretenir d'une chose à laquelle Enoch attachait un prix infini. . . ."
Then Annie with her brows against the wall Answered "I cannot look you in the face; I seem so foolish and so broken down.	"Alors Annie, les yeux baissés et détournant la tête, répondit: Je n'ose vous regarder en face, mon cœur se brise devant tant de sollici-

[1] *Revue de Paris*, Aug. 15, 1868, p. 529.

When you came in my sorrow broke me down;	tude et de bonté, et l'excès du malheur m'a tellement affai-
And now I think your kindness breaks me down;	blie et abattue que je sais à peine comment vous parler.
But Enoch lives; that is borne in on me:	Cependant Enoch vit, j'en suis certaine; à son retour il
He will repay you: money can be repaid;	vous remettra ce que vous m'aurez avancé, on peut s'ac-
Not kindness such as yours."	quitter d'une dette d'argent, mais comment reconnaître tant de générosité?"

There is something natural in the disjointed and abrupt phrases in which Annie expresses her gratitude: in the repetition of the words 'broken down', which seem to obsess her. But in the French all this becomes a formal and well-composed speech of thanks. This translation is not always so stilted, and with two exceptions is free from errors, but on the whole it cannot be called adequate.

Naturally, the *Revue britannique* published a translation, which appeared somewhat tardily in 1877 (July). This simple and pleasant prose version, by Xavier Marmier, follows the text closely, without claiming to reproduce every shade of meaning. In places the expression is unduly prosaic. But Xavier Marmier had, besides a profound respect for Tennyson's poem, a high artistic standard of his own, from which results a definitely satisfactory translation. The publication of the translation by Lemerre ten years later, at a time when so many versions of *Enoch Arden* had appeared, is an indication of the poem's popularity in France.

Three verse translations of *Enoch Arden* were published. The first was in the *Essais de traduction* (1870) of Lucien de la Rive, brother of William de la Rive, literary editor of the *Bibliothèque universelle*.[1] Although the translator took the liberty of altering the poem to his own taste, he is not at his ease in verse; his attempt is marred by poor rhymes. Nevertheless its movement is rapid, free, and vivid. A close comparison of the two poems shows that de la Rive omits many of the details of Tennyson's poem, whilst he emphasises and even invents others. But he works with bold sure strokes, and his poem, though lacking the sobriety and reserve of Tennyson's, has a touching simplicity which is worthy of the original.

But Philip was her children's all-in-all;	Les enfants, eux, s'étaient innocemment donnés:
From distant corners of the street they ran	Vers l'astre de l'amour leurs cœurs s'étaient tournés,
To greet his hearty welcome heartily;	Comme les fleurs des champs après un matin pâle
Lords of his house and of his mill were they;	Tournent vers le soleil leur humide pétale.
Worried his passive ear with petty wrongs	Du plus loin qu'ils voyaient Philippe, ils accouraient;
Or pleasures, hung upon him, played with him	Pour qu'il les embrassât, leurs fronts roses s'offraient;
And called him Father Philip. Philip gained	Leurs voix claires, vibrant d'allègre confiance,
What Enoch lost: for Enoch seemed to them	De leurs chagrins d'enfants lui faisaient confidence;
Uncertain as a vision or a dream,	Puis deux petites mains saisissaient chaque bras,
Faint as a figure seen in early dawn	Et les enfants, sautant de joie à chaque pas,
Down at the far end of an avenue,	Emmenaient entre eux deux, comme un prisonnier, l'homme
Going we know not where ...	Et le conduisaient droit au moulin, leur royaume.

[1] See *Essais de traduction* (Paris, Ch. Meyrueis), 1870.

FORTUNE OF THE LONGER POEMS 71

The translator develops, on his own initiative, this scene of the mill before coming back to the text; even then the two images have only a vague family resemblance:

> La figure d'Enoch, au fond de leur mémoire,
> Se recouvrait déjà d'une teinte plus noire;
> Enoch, c'était quelqu'un dont on ne sait pas bien
> S'il s'éloigne, en marchant sur la route, ou s'il vient.
> C'était un incertain et sombre personnage;
> On ne distinguait pas nettement son visage.
> Et quand on cherchait à le voir pendant la nuit,
> Philippe tout brillant paraissait devant lui.

There is vigour and a spontaneous charm in this: Scherer, whose article in the *Temps* (1870) serves as preface to the book, considers that it has, as well as accuracy, "*le parfum d'un poème original*".

More than any other translator of this poem, Émile Blémont treated it as his own property. He made various arbitrary changes. Annie Lee becomes Annette Lizz; Tennyson gives Enoch credit for three rescues from drowning, therefore Blémont cuts it down to two; Tennyson grants the wedded pair seven years of happiness, and Blémont makes it eight. More important, he saw fit to alter the dénouement of the drama, finding artistic or moral disadvantages in that of the original.

Previously, Blémont had been one of those who professed to despise Tennyson. In 1872 he had devoted to Tennyson one of a series of somewhat superficial articles on Anglo-American literature which appeared in the *Renaissance artistique et littéraire* (May 11). Although here he admires the early poems, and especially the English idylls—"as fresh and bright as a Sussex meadow in spring" —he disparages Tennyson and pokes fun at him in terms shamelessly derived from Taine: "To act as diligent gardener to Nature and the human soul, laying out neat plots where young ladies may stroll, far from the distressing noises and smells of the street, leaning on the arms of their excellent parents, and accompanied by a rich fiancé and a Protestant pastor in a white cravat, all this is no doubt praiseworthy, but it is not what a great poet is for." Either Blémont, as he got to know Tennyson's work better, learned to like it more, or *Enoch Arden* made a special appeal to him, for his translation of the poem shows a remarkable sympathy with its subject. Blémont's *Enoch Arden* appeared serially in *Le Progrès artistique et littéraire* (1885); and when Blémont published his volume of *Beautés étrangères* in 1904, he placed *Enoch Arden* at the beginning of his book.

This translation, although in verse, has one outstanding merit: it equals, or nearly equals, the original in concision. Blémont did not aim at scrupulous accuracy, yet succeeded in retaining all the colour and picturesque detail of Tennyson's poem. Occasionally he intensifies the colour and elaborates the detail to such an extent as slightly to modify the tone of the poem. Compare, for example:

| ... God reward you for it, Philip, with something happier than myself. | ... Et Dieu pour récompense, Vous devrait pour épouse une fleur d'innocence. |

This was, in fact, the fusion of two personalities: now one, now the other, is more in evidence, but generally the fusion is complete and satisfactory, and the translation, for all its independence, maintains an essential accuracy:

| a month—
Give her a month—she knew that she was bound | ... un mois, encore un mois, Pas plus, et ce serait pour la dernière fois. |

FORTUNE OF THE LONGER POEMS

<table>
<tr><td>

A month—no more. Then
  Philip with his eyes
Full of that lifelong hunger,
  and his voice
Shaking a little like a drunk-
  ard's hand,
"Take your own time, Annie,
  take your own time."
And Annie could have wept
  for pity of him;
And yet she held him on
  delayingly
With many a scarce-believ-
  able excuse,
Trying his truth and his long-
  sufferance,
Till half another year had
  slipt away.

</td><td>

Philippe, les yeux pleins de
  cette ardente envie
Qui l'avait dévoré pendant
  toute sa vie,
Répondit, et sa voix tremblait
  comme la main
D'un homme ivre: "C'est
  bon, je passe mon chemin,
Prenez tout votre temps, tout
  votre temps, Annette."
Il lui faisait pitié dans sa
  douleur discrète
Elle le renvoya cependant
  plusieurs fois,
S'excusant mal, pleurant, sup-
  pliant à mi-voix,
Et remettant toujours. Et
  journée par journée
Ils passèrent ainsi la moitié
  d'une année.

</td></tr>
</table>

It is of this essential fidelity that Mallarmé was thinking when he wrote thus to Blémont (October 17, 1885): "The real translation! And how clearly one hears Tennyson's voice singing behind it, if one has the slightest ear for English. I had no need to open the original again, which I expected to do after reading your work; and your verse satisfied me, because it has also, and to begin with, a life of its own."[1]

Obvious proof of this independent existence is seen in Blémont's changing the end of the story to suit himself. In the original, Enoch confides his secret on his deathbed to Miriam Lane, and begs her to tell everything to Annie after his death. In Blémont's version he entreats Miriam

[1] Quoted by Fernand Clerget in his book on *Émile Blémont*, Paris, 1906, pp. 131-132.

to say nothing. It is a strange proceeding, to pay another man's work the compliment of translation, and yet to attempt to embellish it. Yet there is some excuse for Blémont. At first sight it seems surprising that Enoch, after making such a sacrifice for his wife's happiness, should not foresee the unpleasant consequences of a revelation made after his death. Blémont, by making Enoch forbid the disclosure of his secret, wished to magnify his heroism—a dramatic ending which entails only slight modifications in the text. This, in theory, is no doubt the nobler climax; but Tennyson's solution, after all, came nearer to reality. There would be too strict a logic in the prolonging of Enoch's silence after death. In fact, Enoch's is the superior logic. Alive, he would have brought shame and perplexity into Annie's household; the news of his death meant sorrow to her but it would also free her (and Tennyson's public) from the haunting suspicion that she was still living in sin.

Blémont's translation is by far the most interesting of those in verse. The third, by Albert Buisson du Berger, which appeared in the *Bibliothèque populaire Gautier* in 1888, is a good translation which would have been admirable but for the inversions and the padding-out of lines for the sake of the rhyme. One notices a constant effort to reproduce all the original text, including the compound words, impossible to render concisely:

Enoch's white horse, and Enoch's ocean spoil	... Son cheval blanc et, sur la voiture
In ocean-smelling osier, and his face	Dans les paniers d'osier, sa pêche et sa figure
Rough-reddened with a thousand winter gales,	Que les vents de l'hiver rougissaient âprement,
Not only to the market-cross were known,	Étaient familiers sur le marché dormant,

But in the leafy lanes behind the down,	Et dans les longs chemins feuillus au loin derrière
Far as the portal-warding lion-whelp,	La dune, jusqu'au vieux château qu'un lion de pierre
And peacock-yewtree of the lonely Hall.	Défend, dans le jardin qu'un if toujours verdit.

This effort to be exact is often spoilt by useless amplifications required by the rhyme, and in places the general effect is laboured. But, as a rule, Tennyson's poem is rendered in simple and well-chosen language:

So lifted up in spirit he moved away.	. . . Philippe alors s'en fut content,
Then Philip put the boy and girl to school,	Rempli de ce bonheur qu'on a quand on console;
And bought them needful books, and everyway,	Depuis, il envoya les enfants à l'école,
Like one who does his duty by his own,	Leur donna des cahiers, les guida constamment
Made himself theirs.	Tel qu'un père qui fait son devoir ardemment,
	Ne vécut que pour eux. . . .

In 1885 the Conseil de l'Instruction publique added *Enoch Arden* and the *Idylls* to the list of English books prescribed for study in the *rhétorique* and *baccalauréat* classes of *lycées*. This is an honour not usually paid to an author until he has been dead for some considerable time. It helped, no doubt, to make Tennyson more widely known in France, but not, perhaps, more popular.

Some of the translations made after 1885 aimed rather at 'explicating' an author than aiding the appreciation of a poet. That of the Abbé Courtois, for example, is purposely literal: he translates word for word, adding various expressions in italics in order to make quite clear the meaning of the English. The result is no more poetic than the average crib.[1]

A second translation for class purposes, by Émile Duglin, which was published at Beauvais in 1889, is far more dignified. It is accurate and good, as a rule, though from time to time the English master reveals himself in little pedantic phrases. Yet, the best and simplest of all the prose translations, that of A. Beljame (1892), in which, thanks to the discreet sympathy and admirable taste of the translator, every word and idea of Tennyson can be discerned through the French, is also one of those designed for use in schools.

Such, then, was the fortune of *Enoch Arden* in France. The poem achieved success first of all in literary circles, accompanied by various translations in reviews; then came popular editions (the translation of Buisson du Berger in the *Bibliothèque Gautier* cost 10 c. and that of Xavier Marmier in Lemerre's edition 50 c.); finally the recognition of the work as a classic caused it to be extensively known, though in a way which leads us somewhat outside a purely literary survey.

Enoch Arden well bears comparison with attempts made in France to create poetry from the lives of the poor. Émile Montégut, believing, as he did, that the separation of poetry from life was becoming more and more marked, was in this matter the most exacting of critics, but he con-

---

[1] Paris (Poussielgue), 1888, in-16. See, for instance, p. 3: "Alors par un soir doré d'automne, les jeunes gens firent vacances. Ayant en main leur valise, leur sac et leur panier, grands et petits allèrent aux noisetiers chercher des noisettes. Philippe resta une heure en arrière. . . . Comme il gravissait la colline, juste à cet endroit où la bordure inclinée du bois commençait à devenir claire en descendant vers le bas-fond, il aperçut le couple. . . . il s'esquiva et . . . *descendit en rampant* dans les bas-fonds du bois." The vision of Enoch crawling away shows that literalness may be carried too far.

sidered that *Enoch Arden* was "the most successful attempt since *Jocelyn* to bring the realities of everyday life into the domain of poetry".[1]

A most interesting comparison between *Enoch Arden* and *Les Pauvres Gens* of Victor Hugo is to be found in a lecture delivered in the Sorbonne by Charles Dejob in 1900.[2] This critic considers that Tennyson's work is artistically superior to Hugo's. In Hugo's poem there is apparent simplicity, in Tennyson's essential simplicity. "In *Enoch Arden* there is no hint of prearranged and calculated effect. . . . Possibly, when the work has been read, we recollect two or three phrases at most which reveal the skill of the craftsman and which then take on tremendous significance. The composition of *Les Pauvres Gens* is very fine, but also very cunning. One recognises the hand of the seasoned dramatist: everything is arranged to take us by surprise. The poem ends by a phrase led up to with marvellous skill which would bring the applause in a fifth act. Thus we have on the one hand an art which is unconscious and which is concealed, on the other an art which exhibits itself." Tennyson's poem springs from a less facile philosophy than Hugo's: his characters appeal to our sympathy in a more subtle way. Hugo bases the pathos of his story on the more or less commonplace assumption that the dangers of fishermen's lives give them a claim on our pity: whereas the misfortune of Enoch and Annie is *"un malheur qui n'a rien de romanesque . . . ce sont réellement des parias de la destinée"*.

If Tennyson's poetry is distinguished by its art, it must also be given credit for greater sympathy with the suffer-

[1] See *Écrivains modernes*, p. 334.
[2] See *La Revue des Cours et des Conférences*, 1900, p. 751.

ings of the poor. Here the obvious comparison is with Coppée. Coppée, a little later than Tennyson—possibly Tennyson had something to do with this development of his talent—found an original theme in the life of people of humble rank. It can hardly be called an inspiration, for Coppée rather exploits his honest poor. He dwells on the least poetic aspects of their existence; in no way does he feel with them. Rather, he makes his disillusioned grocer, dolefully breaking up his sugar, into an absurd little figure; and gently, but unkindly, ridicules *La Famille du Menuisier*. Whilst Tennyson finds pleasure in the hard rugged character of country-folk as in the *Northern Farmer* (a poem which does not sin through excess of idealism), Coppée sees only the external aspect of his *humbles*. He treats them like a journalist rather than a poet: in depicting them he makes skilful but pitiless use of vulgar little details.

It is possible that *Enoch Arden* strengthened the vogue of the epic of humble life in France. It certainly appealed to a well-established public taste which had already welcomed so many poems of the same kind from *Jocelyn* and *Marie* to *Mireille*; and to that fact it owed its popularity. I can trace only one work inspired by *Enoch Arden*, the theme of which is, of course, traditional, variations of it being seen in the old Breton song *"Quant le marin revient de guerre Tout doux . . ."*, as well as in Maupassant's story *Le Retour*. It was probably Tennyson's poem which suggested to André Theuriet the plot of *Jean-Marie*, a one-act play produced at the Odéon in 1870. The *Revue britannique* assumes this to be so: "Nothing could be purer or more laudable than *Jean-Marie*, and nothing at the same time less fitted for the theatre. It is a Breton elegy of the greatest simplicity. *Jean-Marie* is one of those poems which can be sung, if need be, but not acted; and as far as that goes, I believe that Tennyson's poem *Enoch Arden*, whence M. Theuriet seems to have taken the idea of his piece, would stand acting better."[1] We know that Theuriet was acquainted with Tennyson's poetry: even if he had not read *Enoch Arden* in English, there had been translations in 1868 and 1870, so that the date supports the idea of an adaptation of Tennyson. In many details *Jean-Marie* resembles *Enoch Arden*.[2] It is thus that Thérèse, the young woman, tells of her childhood and betrothal:

> Jadis, sur le chemin qui mène aux Trois-Étangs,
> Un jeune homme habitait dans une pêcherie;
>
> .   .   .   .
>
> Mes parents l'accueillaient, nous grandissions près d'eux
> Ayant même plaisir, même peine, et tous deux
> D'une pure amitié nous sentant l'âme prise,
> Plus tard nous nous étions fiancés dans l'église,
> Or Jean-Marie était fort pauvre, moi sans dot,
> Et dès qu'il eut vingt ans il devint matelot. . . .
> Un jour il s'embarqua pour les mers du Japon.

(Not China.) Jean-Marie's ship goes down with all hands. Thérèse loses all hope of seeing him again and consents to marry Joël, who has been kind to her dying mother. Joël is a farmer, and one day when he goes to market to sell his wheat, Jean-Marie returns and tells his story of the shipwreck, the reef, the desert island, the burning sun, the horror of the lonely nights, and of the ship which at last rescues him. He beseeches her to let him live, even in hiding, close to her:

---

[1] *Revue britannique*, Oct. 1871, p. 528. *Jean-Marie* was published by Gautier in 1871.

[2] In an article written on Tennyson's death, Theuriet praises *Enoch Arden* and *Mariana*, while disparaging Tennyson's work in general (*Le Journal*, Oct. 17, 1892).

> Laisse-moi vivre auprès de toi. Qu'à l'horizon
> Je puisse apercevoir le toit de ta maison;
> Et parfois en passant, voir à travers les branches
> Des noisetiers, flotter ta coiffe aux ailes blanches.

But Thérèse doubts her own strength and begs him to go, which he does, before Joël's return. The resemblance between the two stories is obvious: but Theuriet, whilst borrowing the theme from Tennyson in the first place, made an attempt to develop it on original lines.

Maud, in some ways the sincerest and most vigorous of Tennyson's poems, the one which he himself generally chose to read aloud to his friends, which Taine most admired and which Mallarmé preferred, has been only once translated into French, and that with no very happy result. The author was Henri Fauvel, a provincial doctor, whose hobby was verse and who had steeped himself in English poetry. In his leisure he made translations for the *Nouvelle Bibliothèque populaire*. He was insane, or supposed to be, and later on spent several months under restraint. He was the very man whom Tennyson's enemies would have chosen to put into French the hallucinations of the hero of *Maud*. Fauvel, quite young at this time, lived at Havre, and was not the only poet whose eyes looked across the Channel. Perhaps the idea of translating *Maud* was suggested to him by Jules Tellier, his friend and senior by several years, who tells us how he lived for a long time:

> Dans un recoin perdu des côtes de la Manche
> Avec deux livres: *Maud* et l'*Édel* de Bourget,

reading Tennyson on the shore, near a little fishing port which no doubt reminded him of Enoch's village.[1]

---

[1] *Les Brumes*, 1883 (Lévy frères), *La maisonnette au bord de la mer*. Tellier, as Paul Guigou tells us in the preface to Tellier's *Reliques*, used to

Fauvel's translation, published by Lemale at Havre in 1892, some months before Tennyson's death, is in prose. He adds a preface in verse which, poor as it is, shows how he loved the imaginative and idealist qualities of the poetry of Shelley, Keats, Browning, and Wordsworth; "but of all those dreamers, who . . . like demi-gods, have towered above our age", Tennyson stirred him most:

> Le plus haut, le plus pur et le plus inspiré,
> Celui dont toute l'âme est la splendeur du Vrai . . .
> Est le maître accompli dont j'ai pieusement
> D'une fidèle main traduit le sentiment.

It is clear from the quotations made by Fauvel in his preface that he was well acquainted with Tennyson's work and found in it real inspiration.[1] He apologises for having chosen to translate the gloomiest of Tennyson's poems, which appeals to him because it expresses the sufferings of a heart embittered by the ills of the age, yet struggling to find health.

It is a pity that this sincere homage to Tennyson should take the form of a work in which the faults are only too obvious. Fauvel's knowledge of English was distinctly

---

recite long passages of Tennyson. *Médaillon* in *Les Brumes* is reminiscent of Tennyson; compare also:

| "Sors de toi, cœur malade, et regarde les choses,
 L'analyse stérile enfin doit te lasser."
 (*Les Brumes*, p. 82.) | "It is time, O passionate heart and morbid eye,
 That old hysterical mock-disease should die."
 (*Maud*.) |

[1] See in *Les Dernières Poésies*, de Fauvel, a paraphrase of Tennyson's *Crossing the Bar:*

> " Je puis compter franchir la Barre,
> La grande vague qui sépare
> Du terrible Océan divin—
> Et sans peur de l'ombre qui flotte,
> Sous l'Étoile du Soir enfin,
> En face aborder mon Pilote."

shaky. He follows with patience the tender reveries and choleric outbursts of the unfortunate lover, and often succeeds in reproducing every shade of thought. Yet from the opening stanzas occur elementary blunders in translation which could have been avoided at the cost of a little trouble. Thus, "The wind like a broken worldling wailed" becomes "*Le vent gémissait comme un petit monde qui se brise*": and "He lies and listens mute" becomes "*Il (le rat) ment et écoute*", etc. Examples could be multiplied at will. Along with these inaccuracies can be found really successful passages in which the morbid despair of the hero is interpreted with real understanding:

> Peut-être ce sourire et cette voix tendre venaient-ils d'une pitié bien féminine, car ne suis-je pas, ne suis-je pas ici seul, de longs étés, depuis qu'elle mourut, ma mère qui était si gracieuse et si bonne? Je vis seul dans une maison ensevelie dans le bois sombre, où j'entends à midi les gémissements des morts, et la souris qui s'échappe des boiseries en criant, et mon triste nom résonne dans les coins, quand le frémissement des feuilles agitées frissonne dans les vastes pièces; si bien que j'ai été pris d'une haine et d'une horreur maladives pour un monde que je n'ai encore vu qu'à peine, et qu'une plante parasite et morbide s'est fixée sur mon cœur à demi pétrifié (p. 24).

Here is the obsession of Maud's cold sweet face:

> Mais la lumière crue rayonne et s'abat, et le fantôme flotte et s'enfuit et ne veut pas me laisser en repos: et je hais les jardins et les rues, et les visages qu'on rencontre, les cœurs qui n'ont pas d'amour pour moi; toujours le désir fou me prend de me glisser dans quelque caverne profonde et calme, pour pleurer, pleurer, pleurer, et t'envoyer toute mon âme dans mes larmes (p. 84).

And the call to action:

> Et la pensée noble sera plus libre sous le soleil, et le cœur d'un peuple battra d'un seul désir; car la paix, que je ne re-

gardais pas comme une paix, a cessé, et maintenant le long de la Mer Noire et la Baltique profonde, sous les gueules menaçantes et mortelles de la forteresse, flamboie la fleur de la guerre, rouge de sang, avec un cœur de feu (pp. 95, 96).[1]

[1] The influence of *Maud* will be considered later in connection with Bourget. A little essay, *Du roman en vers,* by Maxime Formont (Bar-sur-Aube (Lebois), 1885), is not without interest. The author considers that Tennyson's poem is a model of its kind, and has nothing but praise for Tennyson's method: "a sort of perpetual monologue which passes through every conceivable modulation. . . . Thought and feeling are recaptured on paper. . . ." He mentions *Francine,* by Édouard Grenier (1884), as an attempt in this genre much inferior to Tennyson's poem.

CHAPTER V

EVOLUTION OF CRITICISM: THE PRE-SYMBOLIST CRITICS

FRENCH critical opinion of Tennyson underwent constant revision. Far from accepting ready-made judgments, those critics who were interested in English literature took pains to survey his work from fresh points of view. We note a marked reaction against the more hasty conclusions of Taine. "Poor Tennyson has no luck", exclaims Edmond Scherer in 1876: Scherer does not forgive Taine for his ill-considered verdict on *In Memoriam*, nor Laprade for his disdainful attitude. "Fortunately, *In Memoriam* is not a poem that can be read hastily, so that these gentlemen probably have the excuse that they only half understood it," he says. "Fortunately, also, we are beginning to judge English literature with a little more understanding of its true genius." [1] To support his view, he quotes a few sentences from a lecture given at Guernsey by Paul Stapfer.[2] The latter, by way of concluding a paper on Musset, salutes two great living poets, Hugo and Tennyson, and says of the second: "He is no doubt engaged in slowly elaborating one of those antique, philosophical poems which elude the understanding of the vulgar, but in which a small number of choice spirits perceive, behind their elegance of form, such depth and such range of thought, that Shakespeare alone in England seems to

---

[1] See *Études*, tome vi. 1876.   [2] March 25, 1868.

them definitely greater than Tennyson." Scherer thus comments on the comparison: "Shakespeare is certainly a great name: it doesn't matter, the Philistines are duly warned!"

The contemptuous tone is still heard. Léo Quesnel's knowledge of Tennyson in 1873 was such as to allow him to believe that *Maud* was the hero's name—"*Maud le fou, Maud l'hypochondriaque amoureux*". He considers that Tennyson may be interesting to study, but is "very little to our taste, and, to speak bluntly, most boring to us nineteenth-century Frenchmen".[1]

But most writers attempt a more serious estimate. Augustin Filon, in a long article in the *Revue des Deux Mondes* of September 1885, observes that since the criticisms of Taine and Montégut the range of Tennyson's work has doubled, and that a second or even a third Tennyson has come to light. This is doubtful. Taine certainly had written before *Enoch Arden*, but Montégut expressed his admiration of that work. And since *Enoch Arden*, Tennyson had published his '*impossible théâtre*', about which his more generous critics kept quiet,[2] *Ballads and other Poems* (1880), *Tiresias and other Poems* (1885). In

---

[1] See *Revue bleue*, 2nd sem. 1873, p. 517; *La Poésie contemporaine en Angleterre* and *Le Correspondant*, Jan.-March 1878; *La Poésie au XIXe siècle en Angleterre*. Another criticism of the same tone is found in *Une Crise de la poésie*, by L. Étienne, in the *R.D.M.*, May 15, 1868, and there is a very odd analysis of *Locksley Hall* in Odysse Barot's *Littérature contemporaine en Angleterre* (Paris, 1874).

[2] The plays were however taken quite seriously in France: notices appeared in the following reviews:

Revue britannique: *Queen Mary*, July 1875, April 1876; *Harold*, Jan. 1877; *The Cup*, Jan. 1881; *The Promise of May*, Nov. 1882.

Revue bleue: *Queen Mary*, Oct. 21, 1876, May 27, 1877; *Harold*, 1st sem. 1882, p. 831, 2nd sem. 1881, p. 352; *Théâtres étrangers*, 2nd sem. 1882; *Le Théâtre anglais contemporain*, 1st sem. 1883; *Becket*, 2nd sem. 1884; "*The Foresters*" *à New York*, 1st sem. 1892; *Un Drame de Tennyson*, 1st sem. 1893.

Bibliothèque universelle: *Queen Mary*, Oct. 1876; *Harold*, Feb. 1877. See

these volumes of his maturity, poems like *Rizpah* or *Locksley Hall Sixty Years after* sound a graver note and bear the mark of a firmer and more vigorous touch; yet they are but a variation of the familiar Tennysonian music and thought. Nevertheless, in critics who wrote between 1880 and 1890, who certainly had not the authority of their predecessors Taine and Montégut, we find a better understanding of Tennyson. There are two reasons for this. First, the logical evolution of Tennyson's talent— for in his case every long poem is the development of some germ readily perceptible in his earlier work— allowed these later critics a more balanced general survey. The effect of the highly wrought fantasies of the *Juvenilia* had been somewhat to distort the perspective of earlier criticisms. It seemed possible to characterise Tennyson's poetry, once and for all, as a lovely but empty work of art; so that *In Memoriam*, *Maud*, and the *Idylls* were judged with a certain amount of bias. *Enoch Arden* revealed an aspect of Tennyson's genius which did not accord with the earlier judgments. Poems like *The Grandmother* and *Rizpah* were proof enough that inspiration from more human sources was neither affected nor a mere passing phase. Interest was aroused, people began to read and estimate afresh poems like *In Memoriam* and the *Idylls*, which, judged on their intrinsic merits, were found to have a significance hitherto unsuspected.

The second and more important reason is that the French literary spirit was undergoing a considerable change. About 1880, words like '*cosmopolitisme*' and '*euro-*

---

also the third of a series of articles on Tennyson by H. Jacottet, May 1888, pp. 310-313.

Revue contemporaine: *Becket* (signed G. S.), 1885, p. 142.

Le Temps: "*The Foresters*" *à New York*, suppt., April 10, 1892.

péenisme' began to appear frequently in literary discussion. The younger men, sick and surfeited with realism, naturalism, and Parnassian poetry, were turning, some towards Wagner and mysticism, some towards Tolstoy and the Russian novelists, others towards the idealism of English poetry. They now had a fraternal kind of interest in English literature; they found it morally refreshing; they saw reflected in it their own agitation, their own aspirations, their own nostalgia. Those who sought purity and moral elevation (mainly absent from their own contemporary literature) were apt to find great charm in Tennyson, whose fame grew by reason of this new and closer sympathy. His idylls of humble life, to take only one example, offered a striking contrast with the Parnassian or realist method of treating similar subjects. "Coppée keeps towards his *humbles*", says Jules Tellier in *Nos Poètes*,[1] "a peculiar tone of ironical and indulgent superiority. . . . How far he is from the simple and profound cordiality of the English poets, and what an instructive parallel one might make by comparing the *Petit épicier* and Tennyson's poem *The Grandmother*." Zola had boasted that his books were the first which really had '*l'odeur du peuple*'. "But if the populace has its odour", exclaims Augustin Filon, "it sometimes has its fragrance. It is that fragrance which we breathe in books like *Geneviève* and *Enoch Arden*." Filon would like to see the *Idylls* and *In Memoriam* discussed in the Sorbonne, so that their faith and idealism might bear fruit among the rising generation. "They would send forth rays which would lighten the darkness where struggles, devoured by pessimism, our sterile youth, and would give it, perhaps, not only the courage to live, but the strength to create."

[1] Paris (Despret), 1888, in-16, pp. 57, 58.

Filon, no doubt, is prejudiced in Tennyson's favour, but his adulation is representative of a definite current of ideas. In the reaction against positivism, against the materialistic outlook which had governed French life and letters for nearly half a century, young men like Gabriel Sarrazin, Édouard Rod, Paul Bourget, Henry Bérenger, and, later on, Gabriel Mourey [1] and André Chevrillon, were influenced above all by English literature. It inspired them to enthusiastic and fruitful pioneer work in criticism like the *Études anglaises* of Bourget or the *Renaissance de la poésie anglaise* of Sarrazin. The accusation that they were untrue to national tradition was quite irrelevant; and this was something more than a literary fashion. They were writers who, stifling in the vitiated air of realism, needed some purer, more quickening intellectual atmosphere in which they might draw upon their innate strength.

M. Henry Bérenger, who shared the state of mind of what he calls '*la période de l'attente de l'idéalisme*' (1880–1887), is probably swayed by personal preference in assigning to Tennyson a preponderating influence at this time.[2] He and his contemporaries drank deep at the springs of English poetry, which, he believes, is in all its phases—pantheist in Shelley, moralist and Protestant in Wordsworth, idealist and heroic in Tennyson—essentially aesthetic. "Adorable figures of Tennyson and Shelley", exclaims Bérenger in his article on Sarrazin, "you whose supernatural beauty is but the outward splendour of an

[1] M. Mourey is not attracted by Tennyson: in *Passé le détroit* (Paris, 1895) he speaks of "the false grandeur of Tennyson".
[2] See in *L'Aristocratie intellectuelle* (Paris, Colin, 1895), *Le Nouvel Idéalisme*, where he deals with the initiators of "the cult of Tennyson, Tolstoy, Browning, Dostoïevsky, Wagner, and Ibsen". Again, in an article on Sarrazin he gives the place of honour to Tennyson (*L'Ermitage*, 1st sem. 1894, p. 323).

inner morality which is perfect, are you not the very image of that Poetry, of that Soul?"

For some critics Tennyson's work has less importance than that of Shelley or the Pre-Raphaelites. Édouard Rod, for example, a fervent Anglophile under whose editorship the *Revue contemporaine* showed such eager hospitality towards English literature, does not write on Tennyson. In the first volume of the *Revue contemporaine*, however, one finds this defence of Tennyson: "People are in general apt to look on Lord Tennyson as a creator of exquisite clouds of gold (opinions expressed in France by MM. Taine and Scherer). They forget that *Maud*, *In Memoriam*, and, above all, *Rizpah* are works worthy of a man and are not merely the vaporous musings of a dreamer. *Rizpah* especially, a magnificent storm of terror and pity, as it thunders forth its music, is in the true domain of sorrow and of life." [1]

Not one critic of this period sees in *In Memoriam* or the *Idylls* the work of a mere dilettante. Not all admire the poems for the same reasons or in the same way, yet they all agree in refuting the judgment of Taine upon them.[2] Augustin Filon writes of *In Memoriam* with profound respect and in absolute sympathy. He represents it as the drama of the poet's faith which, shaken at the beginning, harassed by distress and clouded by ignorance, in the end shines forth clear, sure, and triumphant. The poem con-

---

[1] In Rod's *Morceaux choisis des littératures étrangères* (Paris, 1899), Tennyson's work is well represented by prose translations of *The Lady of Shalott*, *The May Queen*, *In Memoriam*, xxxiii., *The Passing of Arthur*, and *Tears, idle tears*.

[2] See the review by Filon of Sarrazin's *Renaissance de la poésie anglaise* in the *Revue bleue*, 1st sem. 1890, p. 149. A critic of the *Indépendant littéraire*, reviewing the same book, notes that on the subject of Tennyson Sarrazin breaks away from Taine, and adds: "Tennyson is obviously one of the foreign poets who most appeal to our national mind. He has exactly that charm, delicacy, and enthusiasm which enchant us" (May 15, 1889).

sists not of a string of arguments and refutations, but of fears and aspirations which come into conflict and succeed one another like sunshine and shadow. He insists on the sincerity of the poem, and reminds his readers that this conversation with a dead man lasted for ten years. "Does one devote ten years of one's youth to a mere literary fiction?"[1] He emphasises the symbolical side of the *Idylls*, seeing in Arthur not only the ideal of a society, but the better soul of humanity. "His struggles are those of the spirit against the flesh. With its defences broken down on all sides, and apparently beaten, the soul finally triumphs...."

Gabriel Sarrazin interprets Tennyson's work in much the same way.[2] For him, that work vibrates with moral and even social significance. He is astonished that Taine saw little in the *Idylls* but the work of a great poet-archaeologist. Like Taine, he admires their impeccable art—here, for once, he notes, English art rivals and even surpasses that of France—but he sees in them, besides a work of art, "*un puissant coup d'aile vers le sublime*. An ideal, both mystic and moral, is present throughout: there is no need to search or go deep: it shines as clearly as possible behind the veil of diaphanous lace-work...." He finds in the *Idylls* "generous and magnificent thoughts, those of a superior and fruitful Christianity", represented by the nobility and generosity of Arthur, the submission of Enid, the pure love of Elaine, and the immaculate holiness of

---

[1] See the article in the *R.D.M.*, 1885, already quoted. An answer to Taine's criticism seems to be implied in these words. In a later article Filon makes a direct allusion to Taine's impatience: "How regrettable it is that M. Taine did not take the trouble to understand *In Memoriam*. He thus deprived himself of the good fortune of penetrating to the inner sanctuary of Tennyson's genius" (*Journal des Débats*, Oct. 11, 1892).

[2] His study of Tennyson in *La Renaissance de la poésie anglaise* (1889) first appeared in *La Nouvelle Revue*, Dec. 15, 1888.

Galahad. Sarrazin points out how true holiness leads to action. He considers the whole to be "one of the noblest poems in existence, at once lofty and broad, mystic and human".

It must be granted that Sarrazin is carried away by his enthusiasm. Tennyson in the *Idylls* tried to give expression to such aspirations, but his is not the burning passionate idealism that Sarrazin understood it to be.

Taine, with all his science and positivism, never realised how extremely Victorian Tennyson was. He had missed countless modes of thought and expression, both conscious and unconscious, which connect Tennyson closely with the ideas, illusions, and aspirations of his time. Taine had been content to set him down as a dreamer who deliberately stood aside from the contemporary intellectual movement.

Sarrazin, who perceived all through English poetry "the sob of human aspirations, the great voice, confused, as yet, of future humanity", no doubt exaggerated Tennyson's importance as the spokesman of his age, but he established a fact which seems to have escaped his predecessors. He devotes an entire section of his study to Tennyson as a poet of modernity and real life, and to a consideration of his philosophic views. In *Locksley Hall*, admired by Taine simply as a poignant cry of passion, he rightly sees a reflection of the splendid vision of hope which shone before England at the Reform of 1832. The personal theme of *Maud*, in which Taine likewise admired the vehement expression of disappointed love, stands out from a background very characteristic of the days in which it was written: in 1855 people had realised that peace and progress were not bringing about the millennium dreamt of, and the general attitude was tinged with sarcasm and revolt.

Sarrazin thus sees in all Tennyson's poetry the repercussion of the thought and conscience of his age, and a continual preoccupation with the social, scientific, and psychological problems of modern life.

The truth appears to lie somewhere between the views of Sarrazin and of Taine. Tennyson, without expressing any novel or particularly interesting ideas, always strove to identify himself with current thought, to which he tried to give poetic, if not philosophic or scientific shape. To some, this vague expression given by Tennyson to contemporary ideals is the only kind compatible with true poetic inspiration. Émile Hennequin, writing in the *Revue indépendante* (January 1888) on *Le Poétique et le Prosaïque*, assigns to Tennyson, Shelley, Victor Hugo, and Lamartine the highest rank, precisely because their poetry is characteristically vague and idealistic. In his view, poetry properly so-called is neither didactic nor psychological: so that he places the poetry of Heine, Baudelaire, or Byron "in a poetical, if not a literary sense, below the great lyrical effusions of those masters of true impersonal and ideal poetry".[1]

The original writings of these idealist critics give evidence of the sympathy which they felt for the English poets. In the *journal intime* of Gabriel Sarrazin, *La Montée*, part of which was written in England (1878-79), there are various glimpses of landscapes in the Tennysonian manner with analyses of a state of mind strongly resembling that of the hero of *Locksley Hall*. Henry Bérenger, who made a good prose translation of *The Poet* for *La Plume* of November 1892, counts himself, as he writes in the pre-

---

[1] See also Antonin Bunand, *Petits lundis*, 1890, p. 235: "Even a pure artist like Tennyson . . . has more than once steered his bark full into the current of modern life."

face to his volume of poems, *L'Ame moderne* (1892), among "those who have felt the beatings of the great troubled heart of this century, who have loved its painful but magnificent efforts, whose vision has steeped itself in the sights and passions of the modern world—Elizabeth Barrett Browning and Alfred Tennyson in England, Walt Whitman in America". Bérenger feels drawn towards some ideal land:

> Et pourquoi n'est-il pas une métempsychose
> Qui nous puisse pousser vers toi, puisque tu mets
> Dans nos yeux ces reflets d'exil, *ces pleurs sans cause,*
> O patrie inconnue où nous n'irons jamais!
> <div align="right">(<i>L'Ame moderne</i>, p. 24.)</div>

Unlike the orthodox symbolist, Bérenger believes in action and in the continuity of progress: he has faith in the discoveries of mankind: and his verse is an attempt to reconcile poetry and modern life. It is not a successful attempt, but is interesting inasmuch as it has analogies with *Maud* and *Locksley Hall*, and even in expression reminds us at times of those poems.[1] As a poet and artist, Bérenger is not to be compared with Tennyson. His verse is laboured, and, though treating of the newer aspects of civilisation, does so in decidedly conventional idiom. Tennyson, wishing to refer to the new railways, did so in a striking, if inaccurate, image:

---

[1] Compare:

"Ah, je puis donc enfin vibrer avec ma race Et lui dire des mots où nous soyons d'accord. Je puis être poète avec la foule encore, Puisque ceux de ma race ont la foi que j'embrasse." (*Le Chant de la tour*, p. 112.)	"I have felt with my native land, I am one with my kind, I embrace the purpose of God, and the doom assigned." (*Maud*.)

Let the great world spin for ever down the ringing grooves of
    change,

which, as we learn from a note of his, came to him during his first train journey from Manchester to Liverpool. Bérenger simply describes a locomotive in verse; he chants a hymn to the Eiffel Tower, and one poem, on a sunset behind the Institut, was bad enough to gain slight notoriety.

Tennyson's poetry plays an amusing part in the first of the *Amours anglais*, a collection of short stories by Augustin Filon.[1] Gerard, a model young baronet, falls in love with an invalid girl: his love and kindly devotion bring about her cure. But how does he finally win her heart? By reading Tennyson to her. "Avoiding the Gothic visions, the pagan fantasies, and all that savours of the philosopher, the man of learning, the dilettante, Gerard chooses the poems which appeal to young and tender hearts. He reads to her *The Brook*, *The Miller's Daughter*, those chaste and tender idylls; then *The Talking Oak*. Joy is quickly followed by sadness: Ethel and Gerard experience together the exquisite bitterness of *Maud* and *Aylmer's Field*." Under the spell of these emotions their hearts beat as one, and after inevitable misunderstandings have been overcome, all ends happily.

The idealised figures of Tennyson's world haunted another young poet, destined for fame, of whom we speak last in order to make clearer the dual part which he played. We go back to the days when Anatole France and Paul Bourget had written little else but poetry, and when Maurice Bouchor, close on the heels of his friend Bourget

[1] Paris, 1888: see *Le Sanatorium*. See, too, an earlier novel by Octave Feuillet, *L'Histoire d'une Parisienne* (Calmann-Levy), 1881: the misunderstood wife reads Tennyson, "the most chaste of poets"; later on, being disillusioned, "*Jeanne n'est plus romanesque, elle ne lit plus Tennyson*".

in the pursuit of glory, had no reason to fear that the rewards would be unequal. Bouchor, in his *Chansons joyeuses*, tells us how the two friends (Bourget was then only twenty-two) used to meet to read poetry and "*pour boire une discrète et bonne tasse de thé*":

> Et nous relirons encore,
> Le cœur doucement navré,
> Ce douloureux: Never more!
> Que Tennyson a pleuré.[1]

It is charitable to suppose that Bouchor was thinking, not of Poe's raven, but of *Tears, idle tears*.

In Bourget's first volume of poems, *Au bord de la mer*, we find verses inspired by the same poem, and bearing the same title:

> Quand tes yeux ouvriront sur un beau paysage,
> Si le ravissement te fait verser des pleurs,
> Ne retiens pas ces pleurs, mon enfant, sois plus sage
> Et ne te raille pas de ces vaines douleurs.
> Ces larmes sans objet, ces angoisses divines
> Qui nous prennent devant l'océan et les cieux,
> Cette extase sans nom qui court dans nos poitrines
> Comme un frémissement triste et délicieux,
> Tout cela vient du cœur, O mon enfant chérie. . . .[2]

The *petits poèmes* of Bourget, written likewise between 1872 and 1875, show striking resemblances to *Maud*. They are chaste stories, full of the pathos of unrequited love. Their action takes place always at a château, in the most refined surroundings:

> . . . dans le parc d'un ancien château
> Où des cygnes erraient sur une pièce d'eau,
> Ceinte de marroniers gigantesques. . . .
> (*Le Reliquaire*, p. 14.)

---

[1] See the poem, *A Paul Bourget*, in *Les Chansons joyeuses*, Paris (Charpentier), 1874, in-12.
[2] *Poésies* (1872–1876) (Lemerre), 1876, vol. i.

The young lovers all have blue eyes and fair hair, and are excessively dreamy and melancholy. The lover in *Jeanne de Courtisols* commits suicide as he thinks of the radiant face of his fiancée at the ball; she is like another *Maud*:

> Et des perles au front, blanche en robe de soie
> Vous dansez: et quel chaste et virginal émoi!

One is reminded of *Maud* again, or of Amy in *Locksley Hall*, as one reads *George Ancelys*, the story of a young man who dies of love for his cousin, married to his rival. In another poem the very words of Maud's lover are echoed in the passionate cry of a nun who seems to hear the footstep of the man she loved long ago:

> Ce pas à lui, pour moi vivant, et si vivant,
> Qu'on aurait beau me mettre en terre plus avant
> Que tous les morts, du fond de ma fosse muette,
> Au seul bruit de ce pas adoré sur ma tête,
> Je me réveillerais pour l'écouter, ce bruit. . . .
> 			(*Les Deux Nonnes*, p. 206.[1])

Bourget's second volume of poems, published by Lemerre in 1887, contains an adaptation of the song from *Pelleas and Ettarre, A rose, one rose, no other rose had I* (*Un ver dans la rose*, d'après Tennyson):

> Une rose, j'avais une rose, rien qu'une,
> Pâle rose, poussée au pâle clair de lune,

---

[1] "She is coming, my own, my sweet;
  Were it ever so airy a tread,
  My heart would hear her and beat,
  Were it earth in an earthy bed;
  My dust would hear her and beat,
  Had I lain for a century dead;
  Would start and tremble under her feet,
  And blossom in purple and red."
			(*Maud*, xxii. xi.)

> Elle embaumait la terre, elle embaumait les cieux,
> Une rose, ma rose! Elle embaumait ma vie.
> Qu'importaient à mon âme amoureuse et ravie
> Les épines du beau rosier mystérieux? . . .
> <div align="right">(<i>Les Aveux</i>, p. 236.)</div>

In the same volume is a long narrative poem, *Édel*, another story of unhappy love. The heroine is still Nordic, being Danish. In *George Ancelys* Bourget had already experimented with the device of alternating metres. *Édel* consists of short poems written now in octosyllabic lines, now in Alexandrines. The effect of sudden transition thus obtained is good: thoughts are broken off, then taken up again, exactly as in *Maud*. Here is an example of one of these transitions, where the words themselves are derived from *Maud*:

> Oui, j'ai cruellement raison. Mais que c'est triste!. . .
>> Qu'il fût possible seulement
>> Après ce long, ce dur tourment,
>> D'appuyer ma tête calmée
>> Sur le cœur de ma bien-aimée. . . .
>> <div align="right">(<i>Édel</i>, vi. iv., vii. i.)</div>

Like *Maud*, *Édel* is in the form of a monologue, the intermittent record of the phases of an ideal, unhappy love for "*ce doux lys du Nord*." In all these poems of Bourget, love appears in a mystic, somewhat spiritualised form; it is a restless, brooding fever, tinged with vague sadness, 'dark and true and tender'.

"Why does M. Bourget travel?" asks Jules Tellier in *Nos Poètes*. "Is he only half a pessimist? Has he still some illusions left?" After 1880 Bourget made frequent visits to England. How strongly Anglophile he was at a certain period may be gathered from a glance at the *Études anglaises*—the series of essays which recount the pilgrimages made by this '*lakiste parisien*', as Charles Morice called him, in the land of Shelley, Tennyson, Wordsworth, and the Pre-Raphaelites.[1] What precisely attracted him? He admired certain English ideals, but it cannot be said that he was first and foremost a man of ideals. His interests were above all literary and aesthetic. Moreover, he was fascinated by distinction and refinement, whether social or literary, and sought those qualities in the life and literature of contemporary England. To such tastes, work like Tennyson's admirably responded.

In fact, his pilgrimage begins at the Isle of Wight. He goes to Freshwater, where Tennyson lived, and walks on the cliffs near the Needles, whence Tennyson loved to contemplate the stars. Bourget imagines the poet on his nocturnal rambles, and falls to reading him again. He is captivated especially by *The Princess*, which he loves for its English freshness, and for the touch of dreamy melancholy which mingles with its delicate high spirits.

Like Taine, Bourget sees an analogy between the Isle of Wight and Tennyson's poetry. He finds himself here in too civilised a world, where the ugliness of life is so well hidden beneath an exterior aspect of beauty, comfort, and orderliness, that one forgets the existence of the ugliness. "One understands how, among these villas and under this sky", writes Bourget, "the noble and tender poet Tennyson was able to write the *Idylls*, those heroic legends whose beauty harmonises so perfectly with the dreams of this English world, which I like to compare to a flower which wants to forget its stem." He regrets that there is missing from Tennyson's work, as from the

---

[1] *Études anglaises* form the second volume of *Études et portraits* (Paris: Lemerre, 1888). These articles appeared from 1880 onwards in *La Nouvelle Revue* and *Le Journal des Débats*.

delightful Isle of Wight in which he lived, a "corner left over to wildness and freedom".

He is under the enchantment of certain of Tennyson's figures: Mariana, for example, and the girl who sings *Tears, idle tears*. From his readings of English poetry, he had imagined the typical English girl as an ethereal, spiritual creature, sad-eyed and wistful: and in 1880, on his first visit, he was able to see these Tennysonian heroines before his eyes. They are beings full of a mysterious charm. "Looking at these faces, of the idealised beauty that one finds in a Keepsake", he says, "one thinks of fragile creatures. One remembers Shakespeare's Imogen, the lady evoked by Shelley in the garden where quivers the sensitive plant, Tennyson's Mariana sighing alone in the moated grange. . . . One imagines a sensibility as exquisite as that of the maiden whom this same Tennyson describes in *The Princess* as shedding idle tears at the sight of an autumn landscape, tears deep as love—deep as first love and wild with all regret." With an astonishment which is also admiration, Bourget realises that these Marianas in flesh and blood play lawn-tennis.[1]

Bourget quickly communicated to his fellows his impressions of England and his warm affection for English poetry. About him, to some extent, the Anglophiles grouped themselves. It was to Bourget that Sarrazin dedicated his *Renaissance de la poésie anglaise*.[2] Later, Joseph Texte pointed to Bourget as the most distinguished exponent of English ideals of the moment.[3] These ideals he helped to pass on to a new generation of French poets.

---

[1] See *Œuvres de critique*, vol. ii., 1900, pp. 453, 454.
[2] According to Jules Tellier in *Nos poètes*, Henri Fauvel was a disciple of Bourget, from whom the idea of translating *Maud* probably originated.
[3] See *Petit de Julleville*, vol. xviii.: *Relations littéraires de la France avec l'étranger depuis 1848.*

CHAPTER VI

TENNYSON AND THE SYMBOLIST MOVEMENT

THIS generation had, however, ancestors in direct line who themselves had drawn a part of their inspiration from English poetry.

Obviously in the case of Baudelaire Anglo-Saxon influence is almost wholly summed up in Poe.[1] A few images borrowed from Longfellow have been noted—in *Le Guignon*, for instance. There is in *Les Fleurs du Mal* a reminiscence of Tennyson's *Lotos-Eaters* which has not to my knowledge been commented on. To convey the sweet weariness of Lotos-land Tennyson wrote:

> In the afternoon they came unto a land
> In which it seemed always afternoon.

It was this sleepy, sun-steeped landscape which Baudelaire had in his mind's eye when he wrote in *Le Voyage*:

> Nous nous embarquerons sur la mer des Ténèbres
> Avec le cœur joyeux d'un jeune passager.
> Entendez-vous ces voix, charmantes et funèbres,
> Qui chantent: "Par ici, vous qui voulez manger
>
> Le lotus parfumé! C'est ici qu'on vendange
> Les fruits miraculeux dont votre cœur a faim.

[1] See two articles by J. Charpentier in the *Mercure de France*, April-May 1921: *La Poésie britannique et Baudelaire*.

Venez vous enivrer de la douceur étrange
De cette après-midi qui n'a jamais de fin. . . ."
(*Le Voyage*, vii. Strophes 5 and 6.)[1]

Baudelaire thinks very highly of Tennyson. In this he is no doubt following the gospel according to Poe, who said of Tennyson in his essay *The Poetic Principle*: "In all sincerity I regard him as the noblest poet who ever lived, *not* because the impressions he produces are at all times the most profound, *not* because the poetical excitement he produces is at all times the most intense, but because it *is*, at all time, the most ethereal—in other words the most elevating and the most pure. No poet is so little of the earth, earthy." Baudelaire notes this "quasi-fraternal admiration", and contrasts the genius of Poe—"dreamlike in its depth and sheen, crystal-like in its mystery and its perfection"—with "the smooth, harmonious, distinguished melancholy of Tennyson".[2] It is the sombre side of Tennyson's poetry which attracts him. Several times he couples his name with that of his demigod Poe.

[1] Armand Renaud, in an admirable article on Tennyson, "ce poète qui charme et qui ne passionne pas", in the *Revue contemporaine* (vol. xxxv., 1863), points out the analogy between certain of Tennyson's portraits of women, above all *Lilian*:

> "Prithee weep, May Lilian,
> Gaiety without eclipse
> Wearieth me, May Lilian . . .
> Like a rose-leaf I will crush thee. . . ."

and Baudelaire's ideal—"une tête de femme légèrement mélancolique", as in *Madrigal triste*:

> "Sois belle et sois triste! Les pleurs
> Ajoutent un charme au visage."

and *A celle qui est trop gaie*:

> "Et le printemps et la verdure
> Ont tant humilié mon cœur,
> Que j'ai puni sur une fleur
> L'insolence de la nature."

[2] See Baudelaire, *Œuvres complètes* (1870, Lévy), tome vi. p. 22.

"Byron, Tennyson, Poe, and Company. Melancholy sky of modern poetry. Stars of the first magnitude." In violent reaction against "skin-deep" poetry, he sees the future of poetry in this sombre inspiration. He grows indignant at the word 'decadence'. "Why joy always? To amuse us, perhaps. Why should not sadness have its beauty? And horror as well? And everything? And anything?" The author of *Maud* has a place of honour amongst the initiators. "Byron, Tennyson, E. Poe, Lermontoff, Espronceda —*mais ils n'ont pas chanté Margot! Eh! quoi! je n'ai pas cité un Français. La France est pauvre.*"[1] Baudelaire did better than his masters, and enriched French poetry by his powerful originality.

Baudelaire, then, knew and admired the music of Tennyson, and that music must have had some influence upon his efforts to develop the metrical resources of the French language and to exploit that "little-known and mysterious prosody, like Latin and English", which he believed it to possess.

One conquest of Tennyson's might surprise those who slight him—Tennyson's poetry won the heart of Paul Verlaine. Verlaine, in whom were combined two very different beings, might well have chosen to scoff at this well-bred, well-to-do gentlemen, this singer of chaste songs. And yet, through the veil of a foreign language ("*je pioche ferme l'anglais*" is a constant refrain in his later letters),[2] in spite of all the differences of race and temperament, certain poems of Tennyson touched the deepest

[1] See *Polémiques* (Œuvres posthumes, M. de F., 1908): *Lettre à Jules Janin*. Again, in *L'Esprit et le style de M. Villemain*: "He thought of Longfellow, but omitted Byron, Barbier, and Tennyson, doubtless because a professor always inspired him with more tenderness than a poet."

[2] See in *La Correspondance de Paul Verlaine*, tome 1er (Messein, 1922), two letters written at Mons to E. Lepelletier, pp. 135, 147.

and gravest chords in Verlaine's nature. It is the Verlaine of *Sagesse* who loved Tennyson, the Verlaine of those peaceful days in England where in Tennyson's native Lincolnshire Verlaine enjoyed more than one might imagine the calm of an ordered life, respected by others and respecting himself.[1]

Few French poets have lived so long in England as Verlaine: he spent in all three years of his life in England. His first visit in September 1872 was merely a matter of chance. "The other journeys", as M. G. Jean Aubry points out in his excellent article on *Verlaine et l'Angleterre*,[2] "were the result of some deep and varied attraction, the persistence of which is revealed in his work". *Les Aquarelles*, for instance, poems written in London between December 1872 and April 1873, seem surrounded by an English atmosphere: "in this air Verlaine finally freed himself from Parnassian mythology—his simplicity was tempered anew". A second visit comes to an abrupt end in the flight of Rimbaud and the quarrel in Brussels, in which Verlaine shot Rimbaud in the hand, paying for his rashness with two years in prison. On his release, Verlaine, now a fervent Catholic, too sensitive to return to Paris, came to lose himself in the English countryside. Then began, as M. Aubry remarks, not perhaps the happiest period of Verlaine's life, but the calmest, the fullest, and the most dignified, to which we owe his two most moving and beautiful volumes, *Sagesse* and *Amour*. His sojourns in England and their moral and material influence on the

[1] See the account of this stay at Stickney in M. Ernest Delahaye's likeable study *Paul Verlaine* (Messein, 1923), p. 216 *et sqq.*, including the letter quoted on p. 225: "Ma vie est follement calme, et j'en suis si content!"

[2] *Revue de Paris*, 1918, Oct. 15, Nov. 15, and Dec. 1. Marcel Coulon considers this subject in *Les Marges*: *Verlaine anglais*, Feb. 1919, p. 66; *Exégèse verlainienne*, April 1919, p. 222.

mind and habits of the poet are more intimately connected with these two volumes than with any of his other work.[1]

Here, then, is Verlaine at Stickney, teaching French—and Drawing. The very morning after his arrival he meets a certain Canon Coltman, and with his delightful adaptability becomes that clergyman's firm friend. This is how Verlaine tells of the meeting:[2] "When I awoke next morning, very early as usual, I went for a walk in the garden, where I met an old gentleman with a white beard who spoke French tolerably well. . . . I will say, in conclusion, regarding this sympathetic and venerable personage, that he was very well read and very well informed, a friend of Lord Tennyson, and I believe his contemporary at Eton, Oxford, or Cambridge." (One quite understands Verlaine's impression that Tennyson had been to Eton.) The Canon had a great admiration for Tennyson's work, and infected Verlaine with some of his zeal. Verlaine read Tennyson, and contemplated translating a selection of his work. Mr. George Moore tells of a visit paid in later days to Verlaine, who speaks to him of Tennyson, and deeply regrets that he cannot afford to make the journey to ask the Laureate personally for his authorisation of a volume of translations. Moore even went to Macmillan's about it, but the project never took shape, so that, as Moore puts it, Tennyson just missed being translated by a poet greater than himself.[3]

[1] See, in the edition of *Romances sans paroles* in the series *Maîtres du Livre* (Crès, 1923), fifteen poems of English inspiration collected and annotated by M. Van Bever.
[2] In an article in the *Fortnightly Review*, July 1894 (*Notes on England—Myself as a French Master*). The article, which is in English, tells with characteristic geniality of his sojourns in Stickney, Bournemouth, and Lymington.
[3] In *Impressions and Opinions*: (A Great Poet), p. 91.

Verlaine was attracted most of all by *In Memoriam*, which he wanted to translate. Ch. Martrin-Donos, in *Verlaine intime*,[1] quotes what he imagines to be an unpublished original poem in prose. This fragment is actually a translation of *In Memoriam*, civ.: it is dated December 1875. Verlaine found in this poem an expression of his own loneliness:

> Le temps s'approche de la Nativité du Christ—La lune est cachée, la nuit est tranquille. Une seule église, au pied de la colline—enveloppée dans la brume carillonne.
>
> Un seul carillon de cloches en bois—qui éveille à cette heure du repos—un seul murmure dans ma poitrine—Las! ce ne sont pas les cloches que je connais!
>
> Comme des voix d'étrangers elles sonnent—Dans des terres où pas une mémoire ne rôde—ni où une marque ne respire d'autres jours—mais où tout est nouveau terrain, non sanctifié.

Some years later, when, like Tennyson, Verlaine lost a great friend, Lucien Létinois, the peasant boy whom he liked to call his son, he too wrote his *In Memoriam*.[2] The two poems are as different as were the natures of the two poets. Tennyson, reticent even in sorrow, endeavours to prolong the spiritual contact with his lost friend. In Verlaine's poem there is no philosophy, no abstract reasoning; with a very human grief he mourns the merry companion of his daily walks:

> Mon vieux bras dans le tien. . . .

[1] Paris, 1898, p. 102-106. This translation seems to have passed unnoticed, as M. Aubry gives as the only translation Verlaine ever made Byron's *On hearing that Lady Byron was ill*.

[2] *Amour*. Charles Morice, in his *Paul Verlaine* (Paris, 1888), makes this comparison: "There is nothing like *Lucien Létinois* in any literature. That very exquisite English poet, Tennyson, has written *In Memoriam*, verses springing like flowers from a tomb, but they are not so bravely intimate and confidential as these."

With touching simplicity he brings to us the sense of physical loss:

> Mon pauvre enfant, ta voix dans le bois de Boulogne!

Verlaine himself summed up this difference when, towards the end of his life, he explained to W. B. Yeats that he had tried to translate *In Memoriam* "and could not, because Tennyson was too noble, too English, and when he should have been broken-hearted, he had too many reminiscences".[1] And yet there is little doubt that *In Memoriam* inspired Verlaine's *Lucien Létinois*. Mr. Arthur Symons, who knew Verlaine so well, and who speaks of "his immense admiration for Tennyson", is of this opinion.[2] Moreover, its form bears witness to this influence. A series of short poems, detached in appearance, but bound by an inward unity, is just the form chosen by Tennyson for the slow outpouring of his grief. This is how Verlaine's poem begins:

> Mon fils est mort. J'adore, ô mon Dieu, votre loi.
> Je vous offre les pleurs d'un cœur presque parjure:
> Vous châtiez bien fort et parferez la foi
> Qu'alanguissait l'amour pour une créature.

This is not only the spontaneous feeling of a converted Verlaine who, even in his sorrow, blames himself for having loved a mortal being too well; it is a reminiscence of Tennyson:

> Forgive what seemed my sin in me . . .
> Forgive my grief for one removed,
> Thy creature whom I found so fair.

The notion of translating *In Memoriam* dies hard. In the postscript of a letter dated August 16, 1886, to his

---

[1] Yeats recounts this interview in the *Savoy*, April 1896 (*Verlaine in 1894*).

[2] See his article on Verlaine in the *National Review*, June 1892.

publisher Vanier, he asks "in all seriousness" whether, if Vanier cannot undertake to publish himself, he will at any rate help him to find a publisher for a translation of *In Memoriam*.[1] In three different letters from hospital Verlaine asks Vanier for his copy of *In Memoriam* and a big English dictionary, announcing the first time in his telegraphic style—"Require it to finish translation for review that PAYS!" As Verlaine grew older, artistic preoccupations had to give way to more pressing demands. But this translation, which would have had the double merit of honouring Tennyson and enriching Verlaine, never saw the light.

In that curious attack on Victor Hugo, called *Lui toujours—et assez*, which is included in *Les Mémoires d'un Veuf*, Verlaine sets Tennyson much above Hugo. He dismisses all Hugo's work after *Les Châtiments* as *incommensurable, monstrueuse improvisation*, making exception only of a few poems of *La Légende des Siècles*. " *La Légende des Siècles* contains noble epic poems, of which a few, *Le petit Roi de Galice, Éviradnus*, can bear comparison with the Arthurian poems of Tennyson." Verlaine was very ready to discuss Tennyson and Swinburne with young Englishmen like Arthur Symons and W. Rothenstein, who came to pay him their respects at a time when his compatriots somewhat neglected him. He mingled his praises of Tennyson with praises of the English Sunday and the English landscape ("Those Lincolnshire lanes . . .").[2] M. Vielé-Griffin went to see him in a sordid ground-floor room overlooked by the Vincennes railway line, and he too listened to the praises of Lamartine and

[1] See *Correspondance de Paul Verlaine*, vol. ii. (Messein, 1923), p. 50.
[2] See in *The Academy*, vol. li., 1897, F. L.: *Some Memories of Paul Verlaine*; and in the *New Review*, Dec. 1893, an article by Mr. Arthur Symons on Verlaine.

Tennyson.[1] M. Vielé-Griffin, who only knew Verlaine in his serious moments—times when he would say, *"moi aussi, je suis bourgeois"*—tells me that Verlaine once spoke to him of Tennyson as his favourite poet, and recited some of Tennyson's verse to him.

Contemporary critics tended to overlook or belittle this 'anglicism' of Verlaine's, though he himself made no mystery of it;[2] in retrospect it becomes more and more apparent. Verlaine's personality was too strongly marked, his mind too original for this intercourse with England to have left obvious traces in his work. But just as certain traits of his personality grew stronger in the atmosphere of England, so certain of his poetic faculties gained vigour from his contact with English lyricism. For him, English poetry of the past is summed up in Shakespeare, that of the present in Tennyson.

Even more than Baudelaire, Verlaine banished eloquence from his poetry. His lyric power was inborn, but it gained in confidence, sureness, and strength as a result of his English reading and his sojourns in England. As early as 1889 M. Vielé-Griffin, writing under the pseudonym of Alaric Thome in *Art et Critique*, saw the possibility of this.[3] He speaks of the vogue of freer verse, of the theories of Banville, who never dared fully to practise what he preached. Verlaine took up the task where he left off. "M. Paul Verlaine, who had not an academic reputation to lose, was not afraid to trust to his marvellous ear for music: he advanced timidly at first, nevertheless,

---

[1] *Quelques figures symbolistes* in *La Phalange*, July 15, 1908; and *M. de F.*, Feb. 1899, *Désespérance du Parnasse*, in which M. Vielé-Griffin mentions this preference of Verlaine's.

[2] See in *Les Hommes d'aujourd'hui* a reference to the "great Tennyson". Tennyson is also mentioned in passing in Verlaine's *Confessions* (Paris, 1895), p. 108.

[3] No. 26, Nov. 23, 1889, *Les Poètes symbolistes*, p. 403.

as though groping in darkness, emboldened by Banville and by his familiarity with the work of Alfred Tennyson." The opinion of Mr. Arthur Symons on this head is perhaps biassed, but he too notes [1] that Verlaine has brought something new into French poetry, that in his verse "the words themselves sing, as hitherto English verse alone had sung, with perfect independence, with perfect freedom".

Henri Ghéon, in the *Nouvelle Revue Française*,[2] contrasting the '*rire édenique*' of English nineteenth-century lyricism with the "half-oratorical, half-lyrical thunder of Hugo", holds that the song is much more in the English than in the French tradition; and that in recent centuries it has only come to full fruition in France under the stimulus of foreign influence—as in the case of Poe's spell over Baudelaire. "Verlaine had drunk deep of the wine of his own land, and yet heard the song of Tennyson ringing in his ear."

Here, where one is dealing with what is most exquisite in Verlaine's and in Tennyson's work, one cannot, nor does one wish to make any detailed comparison. It is, however, interesting to trace the development of the song in Verlaine—from the frail and delicate poems of *La Bonne Chanson*:

> Avant que tu ne t'en ailles,
> Pâle étoile du matin. . . .

or

> La lune blanche
> Luit dans les bois. . . .[3]

which have an airy grace very characteristic and wholly French, through the transition stage of the *Romances sans*

---

[1] In the article in the *National Review*, 1892, quoted above.
[2] Feb. 1, 1912 (*Les Poèmes*).
[3] *Œuvres complètes* (Messein, 1923), tome 1, pp. 125-128.

paroles with their catchy rhythms and their gay refrains, where Verlaine makes masterly use of repetition; into *Sagesse*, where his songs have a discreet and a riper loveliness:

> Écoutez la chanson bien douce . . .
>
> Les chères mains qui furent miennes. . . .

to the calm gravity of these two written in prison:

> Un grand sommeil noir
> Tombe sur ma vie. . . .
>
> (*Sagesse*, v. p. 272.)
>
> Le ciel est, par-dessus le toit,
> Si bleu, si calme! . . .
>
> (*Sagesse*, vi. p. 273.)

Lastly we find in certain poems written at Stickney and at Bournemouth an open-air vigour:

> L'échelonnement des haies
> Moutonne à l'infini, mer
> Claire dans le brouillard clair,
> Qui sent bon les jeunes baies. . . .
>
> (*Sagesse*, xiii.) [1]
>
> La mer est plus belle
> Que les cathédrales. . . .
>
> (*Amour*.)

It almost seems that there is in these later songs some of the significant reticence of English lyricism, some

---

[1] One poem from *Sagesse* has a very English rhythm; these lines could almost be scanned:

> "Je ne sais pourquoi
> Mon esprit amer
> D'une aile inquiète et folle, vole sur la mer.
> Tout ce qui m'est cher
> D'une aile d'effroi
> Mon amour le couve au ras des flots. Pourquoi, pourquoi?"
>
> (*Sagesse*, vii.)

memory of the sober poignant notes of Tennyson, from the songs of *Maud* to

> Break, break, break,
> On thy cold grey stones, oh sea!

M. Vielé-Griffin believes that Tennyson counted for something in this evolution, and, as Marcel Coulon rather spitefully remarked: "Of our poets, Verlaine is easily the favourite among our neighbours. There is a very good reason for that." [1]

Verlaine was bound to England by very real ties; in the case of Stéphane Mallarmé this affinity was even more strongly marked. In the first place, Mallarmé learnt English in order to read Poe. After several visits to England he found in the teaching of English a means of livelihood which left him leisure enough to devote himself to his search for a new poetry and a new aesthetic.[2] Anglo-Saxon poetry and the genius of the English language profoundly influenced his mind. The experiment of free verse was, according to Camille Mauclair, the outcome of two exterior influences. The influence of Wagner's music set up a desire to break the bonds of tradition: from the point of view of technique, English poems provided the models. "Mallarmé by his sympathy for the Wagnerian aesthetic and by his kinship with English lyricism and syntax", says M. Mauclair, "stood where these two currents penetrating into French literature converged." M. Albert Thibaudet also acknowledges the influence of English poetry on Mallarmé, but he considers that in his researches in assonance and allitera-

---

[1] See the article *Verlaine anglais* quoted above.
[2] See *L'Art en silence*, by Camille Mauclair (Paris, 1901): *L'Esthétique de Stéphane Mallarmé*; and also M. Albert Thibaudet's book, *La Poésie de Stéphane Mallarmé* (Paris, 1912).

tion, Mallarmé merely felt subconsciously that influence. These two critics do not always see eye to eye about Mallarmé, but they agree that he had an *âme septentrionale*.[1] "Mallarmé's system", writes M. Mauclair, "is the outcome of a mind extremely pure, reflective, Northern, inspired much more by the genius of the English or German language than that of the French. . . . He comes very near to Edgar Poe, whom he understood so well; he seems akin, too, to Tennyson and Mr. George Meredith; his lyricism, like Tennyson's, has a certain white smoothness."

Next to Poe, Tennyson attracted Mallarmé most. If the conversations of the famous Tuesday gatherings of the Rue de Rome had been saved from oblivion by a French Boswell, we might have had some fine comments on Tennyson's artistry; but these discussions were never recorded. Mallarmé's own work, so finely wrought, so purified from all contact with reality, eludes comparison with the work of any other poet. Only a bell "*qui roule par la brume*" seems to bring a distant memory of Tennyson.[2] It would be idle to maintain that Tennyson alone counted for much in the new prosody with which Mallarmé was one of the first to experiment:[3] the work of Swinburne, for instance, offers examples of a much bolder technique. But Mallarmé, whose aim was to develop in French verse that *musicalité intérieure* which characterises English poetry, recognised that Tennyson had "a music all his own",[4] a discreet music of infinite resources. It would be strange if Mallarmé, admiring *Maud* as he did, had not found lyric inspiration in this poem. We have only to read the

---

[1] A. Thibaudet, *op. cit.* p. 24.
[2] *L'Azur*: *Poésies de Stéphane Mallarmé* (N.R.F., 2ᵉ édition, 1913).
[3] We note that in the introduction to *Mots anglais* (1878) Mallarmé mentions many other English poets, but not Tennyson.
[4] See p. 134.

apology written by Mallarmé on the Laureate's death to realise his esteem and affection for Tennyson. We remember that, with the exception of a page on Poe, Tennyson is the only Anglo-Saxon poet to be discussed in the *Divagations*.

The Symbolist reviews proper have little to say of Tennyson. He was taken for granted—a great poet.[1] He stood for a certain ideal of beauty and purity, but he was already a little out of date. Moreover, his official status as Poet Laureate, and the fact that he was "done" in schools and colleges, prejudiced the younger men against him. If they sought inspiration abroad, they turned to the less conventional glories of Whitman or Swinburne. There are, however, in the years that precede Tennyson's death, indications that he is by no means forgotten. *La Revue indépendante* of February 1890 mentions Mallarmé's translation of *Mariana*; *Le Mercure de France* in the same year resurrects the translation in its entirety. The second volume of *La Plume* for 1890 includes a poem by Émile Blémont—*Pleurs sans cause*—which bears as its epigraph 'Tears, idle tears', and is obviously inspired by Tennyson's poem. *La Société nouvelle*, a Belgian revue, socialistic and Anglophile, publishes between August and December 1891 [2] admirable prose translations of five of the longer poems—*The Passing of Arthur, The Dying Swan, The Lady of Shalott, The Lotos-Eaters,* and *Locksley Hall*—by Olivier Georges Destrée, who, attracted by the idealism of English poetry, planned an anthology of nine-

[1] Stuart Merrill, in *La Plume* (March 15, 1893), refers to "the demigods . . . les Tennyson, les Rossetti, les Swinburne".
[2] *La Société nouvelle*: August 30, *Le Trépas d'Arthur*; October 30, *Le Cygne mourant, La Dame de Shalott*; Nov.-Dec., *Les Mangeurs de Lotus, Locksley Hall*.

teenth-century English verse, but gave up literature to become a Benedictine monk. His are certainly among the best translations of Tennyson which have appeared in France. He simply puts Tennyson into French without intruding his own personality, without forcing or exaggerating any word or thought. His translations are in prose, in fine supple phrases which seem best fitted to convey the ample Tennysonian rhythm. The authentic music of Tennyson seems to ring in this simple rhythmical prose, as in the song of the Lotos-Eaters: "There is sweet music here that softer falls...."

Il est ici une musique suave, qui tombe plus doucement que les pétales des roses épanouies sur le gazon, que les rosées de la nuit sur les eaux calmes, entre des murs de granit sombre dans une passe luisante; une musique qui se pose plus mollement sur l'âme que des paupières lassées sur des yeux lassés. Il est ici de fraîches mousses profondes....

The translation of *The Passing of Arthur* especially has admirable dignity. The *Nouvelle Revue* for May 1892 contains some graceful translations by Destrée of some of the *Juvenilia*: *Recollections of the Arabian Nights*, *Adeline*, *Margaret*, *Eleänore*, and the sad little song "*A spirit haunts the year's last hours*".

Le Banquet, a revue founded in March 1892 by young writers very much in earnest, one of whose aims was "to familiarise the French public, in a methodical way, with the most interesting of recent developments in foreign art", begins by translating Ibsen and Nietzsche, and then goes on to Tennyson's *Maud*:[1] Jacques Baignières gives a verse translation of "*Come into the garden, Maud*", which,

[1] April 1892, p. 53 (*Maud*, xxiii.). This interesting review, which counted among its contributors Marcel Proust, Henri Barbusse, and Fernand Gregh, lived for hardly a year.

TENNYSON AND SYMBOLIST MOVEMENT 115

without striving for accuracy, succeeds in keeping the atmosphere of *Maud*:

> Toute la nuit la rose alanguie et pâmée
> Entendit l'harmonie et les frissons lointains
> Des violons et des flûtes; et les jasmins
> Balançaient aux balcons leur danse parfumée.
> Mais l'oiseau se réveille en l'aurore embaumée,
> Et quand la lune meurt à l'horizon jauni
> S'approfondit l'écho du silence infini. . . .

Thus Tennyson's work was still in the minds of the generation of Symbolist poets.

It is in their love of legend that poets of the Symbolist period come closest to Tennyson. This legendary poetry is of somewhat complicated origin. Victor Hugo had set the example; and though his favourite legendary themes were neglected, his legendary manner had its echoes.[1] The dominant factor is no doubt the growing influence of Wagner, which reaches its height with the foundation of the *Revue Wagnérienne* (1886), by Édouard Dujardin, with the concerts of Lamoureux, who persisted in conducting Wagner in the face of furious opposition, and with innumerable French studies of the Bayreuth performances of 1886. But in this legendary poetry there is certainly something of Tennyson. It is he who brings to it the Celtic element. Arthur and Guinevere, Merlin and Vivien, and Elaine come to life again side by side with Wagnerian heroes like Parsifal and Lohengrin. Often the two currents intermingle. Thus Verlaine's well-known sonnet *Parsifal*, which appeared in the *Revue Wagnérienne* for January 8, 1886, has two epigraphs, one of which—"Whom Arthur and his Knighthood called

---

[1] In Jean Lorrain, for instance, as we shall see later.

the Pure"—is from Tennyson. Thus to certain romantic minds Tennyson seems like a second Wagner—"Tennyson, fine and sombre, like an etching to hang beside the Dantesque profile of Richard Wagner".[1]

It is thanks to his Pre-Raphaelite illustrators that Tennyson's work still charms the advanced artistic circles. Above all, Burne-Jones' dreaming faces had fired the imagination of a chosen few: his art gave an intense and mystic life to Vivien and the Lady of Shalott.[2] Jean Lorrain, who was one of the first of his generation to come under the spell of Pre-Raphaelite painting, describes himself (in his *Ames d'Automne*, a strange little book of musing memories) at Le Havre with Bourget, both contemplating with emotion a lady who had been to England specially to see Burne-Jones' picture, inspired by Tennyson's *The Sleeping Palace*. "And stupid and fascinated, you had not eyes enough to look at her, nor ears enough to listen to her ... this stranger who read Tennyson."[3]

An Elaine, *d'après* Tennyson, was exhibited by an Englishman, Logan, in the 1895 Salon: a critic of the *Gazette des Beaux-Arts* for 1899 notes that life is still running strongly in these Celtic legends, "the bushes are a-tremble with birds, the streams and woods are full of mysterious and perverse creatures who put to the proof the asceticism of the servants of the Holy Grail".[4] As an example of this he mentions a *Sir Galahad*, after Tenny-

---

[1] *La Plume*, Dec. 15, 1892. Comtesse de Brocélyande: *Pour une amie qui aime le Nord*.

[2] E. Chesnau, in *Artistes anglais contemporains* (Paris: Rouam, 1887), criticising Burne-Jones' *Beguiling of Merlin*, sets painting aside to admire the psychology of Tennyson's Vivien. In quoting the passage from Tennyson which inspired the picture, he makes use of Francisque Michel's translation.

[3] *Ames d'automne* (Paris, 1898, p. 104): *A Bourget*, dated Sept. 1890.

[4] *Gazette des Beaux-Arts*, 1899, 2nd sem. p. 46.

son, by Lucien Monod. Again, it is through the medium of Pre-Raphaelite art that later André Chevrillon falls in love with Tennyson's poetry.[1] And yet Gustave Kahn, in a criticism of Mourey's book of English studies called *Passé le Détroit*, seeking to repudiate the influence of Pre-Raphaelite art in France, lays all this legendary influence at Tennyson's door, and speaks of "certain poetical works too definitely modelled on a Tennyson rather than on a Rossetti" (*La Société Nouvelle, Ier Semestre*, 1895).

Whether through direct knowledge of his work, then, or through a new energy lent to that work by Pre-Raphaelite painting, Tennyson played his part in creating the poetic mood which sought relief from reality, from actuality, in the shadowy realm of legend.

The decadent Jean Lorrain is one of the first to draw inspiration from the Celtic legends. He tells us, in his *Sensations et Souvenirs*,[2] how, being a Northerner, he has always loved "those epic figures of Celtic legend, Guinevere, Melusine, Elaine, Vivien", and this love found expression under the influence of Tennyson. He was curiously impressionable, and many of his themes were borrowed. Mallarmé characterised him as *diamanté d'influence tennysonienne mais spontanément*.[3] He published in 1883 *La Forêt bleue:* this magic forest is peopled with

> Reines au temps d'Arthus et dryades jadis.
> (*Le Pays des fées*, p. 11.)

The legend of Merlin and Vivien especially charms him. *Viviane* (*La Forêt bleue*, p. 15) is based on this, and again in *Brocéliande* he tells of the spell cast on Merlin. His style

[1] *Études anglaises: La peinture anglaise* (Paris: Hachette, 1901). In this essay M. Chevrillon quotes Tennyson frequently.
[2] Paris, 1895, pp. 42, 43.
[3] See *Divagations* (Paris, 1897): *Tennyson vu d'ici*.

has less simplicity, less reserve than Tennyson's, but certain passages give ample proof of its affiliation to Tennyson's poem:

> ... She lifted up
> A face of sad appeal, and spake and said,
> "O Merlin, do ye love me?" and again,
> "O Merlin, do ye love me?" and once more,
> "Great Master, do ye love me?" He was mute.

> M'aimez-vous, ô Myrrdin, m'aimez-vous, puissant maître?
> Implora-t-elle, et lui, les yeux clos, sans paraître
> L'écouter, lui tendait une fleur de glaïeul
> Et les flots de sa barbe étaient comme un linceul
> D'écume où la parole était morte et raidie.
> <div align="right">(<i>La Forêt bleue</i>, p. 82.)</div>

Jean Lorrain makes this flower symbolise Merlin's thought:

> ... Son amour
> Pénètre, embaume, enivre, et pourtant, nuit et jour
> Le glaïeul est muet et fleurit en silence,

a decorative rendering of Tennyson's

> Who are wise in love
> Love most, say least.

Compare also Vivien's answer in the two poems:

> I saw the little elf-god eyeless once
> In Arthur's arras hall at Camelot:
> But neither eyes nor tongue—O stupid child.

> Éros était brodé sur la tapisserie
> Dans la chambre d'Arthus ...
> Mais il n'était qu'aveugle, aveugle et non morose.
> <div align="right">(<i>La Forêt bleue</i>, p. 83.)</div>

Jean Lorrain dreams of romantic castles, "with their pointed roofs all white with turtle doves", where he will live with a *douce comtesse Élaine*.

Ses deux mains au repos ont la blancheur des lys
Et ses fins cheveux d'or semblent poudrés de givre.[1]

Certain poems of the *Forêt bleue* are dedicated to Victor Hugo, and owe as much to *La Légende des Siècles* as to Tennyson's visions of chivalry; but it is surely the last journey of Elaine which inspired *La Petite Ilse* in *L'Ombre ardente*:[2]

>Pleurez, la petite Ilse est morte.
>On l'a mise en batelet
>Tendu de drap noir, à l'ourlet
>Brodé d'argent, comme on porte
>A la cour pour le deuil du roi.
>... un muet
>Veille le corps blême et fluet
>Et la barque entre les deux rives
>Glisse et descend à la dérive.

None of the Symbolist poets drew from these legends any work so considerable as the *Idylls of the King*. The *Idylls* may be a sort of Albert Memorial in verse, but they have in them a symbolism subdued enough not to interfere with the movement of the story, yet strong enough to set the imagination astir and to create its special impression on the mind. M. André Chevrillon, in his *Études anglaises*, notes that in English poetry "vision and thought are interwoven simultaneously on several planes, becoming wider and more general in character ... spreading to the infinite, melting into the mists of confused emotion. What, for instance, is Tennyson's Arthur? Firstly—a poetic living creature with a personality, a physiognomy, a smile, a tone of voice; then—Christian Honour, full of charity and chivalry, the Englishman's ideal; then—a

---

[1] See in *La Forêt bleue*, *La Montée au Château* (p. 77) and *Il passe un bohémien* (p. 96).
[2] Paris, 1897, p. 141.

god, or rather Godhead itself, speaking with the solemn grandeur of Zeus in verse untrammelled, infallible, eternal".[1]

Mallarmé maintains, in his *Pages*,[2] that "the French mind recoils—and in this is loyal to art in its integrity, which is invention—from all legend". Although for a time, under the influence of Wagner, a legendary mysticism became a cult, as reviews like *Le Saint-Graal* (founded by Emmanuel Signoret in 1892), *L'Album des Légendes* (1894), and *Le Livre des Légendes* (1895), testify, this legendary poetry never gained a firm foothold in France. M. René Doumic, however, mentions mystic chivalry as one of the outstanding traits of the new poetry. "Instead of inventing cold allegories, the poet of to-day takes up the old themes of primitive symbols. The modern mind . . . has begun to revolve again in the cycle of the Round Table."[3]

At first it was the spirituality, the mystic meaning of these legends which fascinated: weary of reality, of the ugliness of modern life, poets sought refuge in an ideal world of dreams and aspirations. But what had been an impulse of the soul soon degenerated into a literary pose: the mystic ideal was lost in a gorgeous but monotonous tangle of obscure and complex symbolism.

Let us investigate the part played by the Arthurian legend in the work of certain Symbolist poets. Henri de Régnier and Stuart Merrill were the initiators of this legendary poetry.[4] "*Dieu! que le monde était beau vers 1891*",

[1] *Études anglaises* (Paris: Hachette, 1901, in-16), p. 14-15.
[2] Bruxelles, 1891.
[3] See in the *R.D.M.*, Aug. 15, 1895, *La Poétique nouvelle*. P. Quillard, in *Les Entretiens* (1891, ii. 59), says: "We might win back our lost heritage and not leave the interpretation of the myths created by our ancestors merely to Englishmen and Germans—Tennyson, Wieland, and Wagner".
[4] *Les Marges*, Jan. 15, 1919: *L'Anniversaire de Stuart Merrill*, by Edmond Jaloux.

exclaims Alfred Poizat in his essay *Le Symbolisme*, "*lorsqu'apparurent ces chevaliers du songe, Henri de Régnier et Francis Vielé-Griffin, tels Gauvain et Lancelot du Lac 'rouge encore du baiser de la reine' ".*[1] H. de Régnier's early volumes, *Les Lendemains* and *Apaisement*, were love poems, and purely personal, but gradually his poetry takes up the theme of chivalry: he is a literary Galahad, lifting *une étoile à la pointe altière de son glaive*.[2] In *Poèmes anciens et romanesques* this chivalry has become an obsession:

> Les grands chevaliers d'ombre et de fer, loin des joutes,
> Aux échos du passé, poussière et fol ébat!
> Chevauchent deux à deux lavés par les absoutes
> Vers le sang des graals et l'espoir du combat.[3]

Then in a rich setting, thrown into relief by the obscure symbolism which H. de Régnier affected at that time, there rises the sad face of Elaine:

> L'usurpateur mystérieux des destinées,
> L'Involontaire Amant qui chevauche et guerroie
> A disparu dans l'ombre au détour des années. . . .
>
> Il a vu, stricte banneret de l'oriflamme,
> Un masque douloureux pleurer parmi les nues
> Du couchant saccagé comme une ville en flamme.
>
> Le pennon et le glaive hauts en ses mains fortes,
> Il traversa le val et la mer et la plaine
> Et vit un soir la ville et les murs aux sept portes
>
> Et sur la tour de marbre fruste, assise, Élaine. . . .[4]

---

[1] *Le Symbolisme* (*Renaissance du livre*), 1919, p. 133. See also introduction, p. 7.
[2] See the introductory sonnet of *Épisodes*.
[3] *Poèmes anciens et romanesques* (1887–1889), Paris, M. de F., 1890, p. 19.
[4] *Ibid., Salut à l'Étrangère:* compare Tennyson's *Elaine*:

> "High in her chamber up a tower to the east . . .
> Till as he traced a faintly-shadowed track,

The art of Henri de Régnier did not for long remain under the yoke of this laboured symbolism: in *Épisodes* (1888) he begins to come under the spell of ancient Greece: *Les Jeux rustiques et divins* (1897) are entirely of Greek inspiration. By a rather amusing transformation the Élaine of *Salut à l'Étrangère* becomes in a later edition Hélène, though the poem remains otherwise unchanged.[1]

Two Americans, Stuart Merrill and M. Vielé-Griffin, formed a living link between Anglo-Saxon and French poetry. "You too", wrote Stuart Merrill to Vielé-Griffin when he began to write in French, "are trying to give to France the Swinburnian song." There is something of Tennyson's manner also in the verse of Stuart Merrill. *Le Palais désert*[2] seems reminiscent of *The Princess*—there is the same languorous hushed garden where waters gleam and white peacocks droop:

> Now sleeps the crimson petal, now the white.
> Now winks the gold fin in the porphyry font. . . .
> Now droops the milk-white peacock like a ghost.

> That all in loops and links among the dales
> Ran to the Castle of Astolat, he saw
> *Fired from the west*, far on a hill, the towers."

P. Quillard, criticising *Premiers poèmes*, considers M. H. de Régnier most closely related to Racine and Tennyson (*M. de F.*, Feb. 1899, p. 459).

[1] *Poèmes*, 1887–1892 (*M. de F.*, 1895, p. 46). Only this poem and the preceding one:

> "Masque pâle sans au front une pierrerie
> Ni funèbre laurier au delà de la mort;
> Quelle parole est morte à la lèvre meurtrie
> De quel aveu pour que la lèvre en saigne encor!"

have any clear connection with the Elaine of the Tennysonian legend: all further analogy is lost in a maze of symbols. H. Spiess, a Swiss poet much influenced by Henri de Régnier, wrote four poems on Elaine:

> "Candide au milieu d'aromes troublants
> et le cœur gonflé d'aveux qu'il doit taire."

[2] Stuart Merrill, *Poèmes*, 1887–1897: *Les Fastes* (*M. de F.*, 1897, p. 91).

> Aucun souffle n'émeut le somnolent silence:
> Les paons sont endormis aux balustres de fer,
> Et dans les bassins roux d'où nulle eau ne s'élance
> Les cygnes, oubliant leur pâle turbulence,
> Rêvent de chants de deuil sous un soleil de fer.

The poem breaks off while a pensive maiden sings of "*son amour éclos et défunt en ce soir*", for a Prince who has died, just as the maidens sang in *The Princess*, as Elaine and Enid sang.

From Tennyson, Stuart Merrill no doubt took the word 'samite', which he works rather hard. In the poem *Conte* he certainly has in mind *The Passing of Arthur*. The resemblance is striking, in spite of the blue dolphins and hippocampi which give to Merrill's poem an extravagantly fabulous air. *Le Héros ingénu sous son heaume d'argent* goes through the world redressing wrongs:

> Or il advint ceci: qu'un soir de vents légers
> Il vint vers une mer merveilleuse de rêve
> Où dans les îles d'or les flûtes des bergers
> Sifflaient. Et laissant choir le fardeau de son glaive
> Il ploya les genoux et sanglota très bas,
> Ses bras de fer en croix et le dos à la grève;
> "Je suis venu mourir, las des mauvais combats
> Au leurre de vos voix lointaines, ô sirènes
> Que pleurent en riant les flûtes de là-bas."

A mystic barque comes to carry away the dying knight:

> Et vers le crépuscule, en ce noble appareil
> La barque déroula son lumineux sillage:
> Et le Héros entra dans l'orbe du soleil—
> Seul, son glaive flambait sur l'argent de la plage,
> Afin qu'un futur Preux, surgissant du millier,
> L'empoignât quelque soir pour en sacrer son âge.
> C'est ainsi que mourut le chaste chevalier.

Again, in *Rêverie*, the sorrowing queen who turns

> Vers le Prince parti pour d'âpres épopées
> Dont l'étendard, parmi la pompe des épées,
> Ondule en plis d'azur purs de toute macule
> Contre l'Or et le Sang d'un dernier crépuscule . . .

recalls Arthur's departure for "that last dim weird battle in the west".

A poet less important in the Symbolist hierarchy, A. Ferdinand Hérold, acknowledges the influence of Tennyson, as well as of Swinburne, on the French poetry of his day.[1] He himself is strongly influenced by Wagner, but in his *Chevaleries sentimentales* (1893) the Celtic legends play their part. Two poems in *Le Livre des Reines* are reminiscent of Tennyson—*Viviane* only vaguely, but *Genièvre* more definitely:

> Le soir de ses cheveux étoilés de rubis
> Elle passe, darde vers le vieux Roi le glaive
> De ses regards aigus, fulgurants et hardis. . . .
>
> Qu'elle est terrible, la belle reine Genièvre.
>
> Près d'elle l'Enchanteur aux doigts mélodieux
> A fait vibrer la harpe d'amour et de rêve
> Et lui suscite un sourire mystérieux.
>
> Qu'elle est étrange, la belle reine Genièvre.
>
> Dans la paix du jardin glorieux et charmé
> Monte un murmure, comme d'une source brève:
> Et c'est la voix palpitante du Bien-aimé.
>
> Qu'elle est joyeuse, la belle reine Genièvre.
>
> (*Chevaleries sentimentales*, p. 43.)

In the *Nuits d'Épiphanies* of André Fontainas, two

---

[1] *Enquête sur les influences étrangères* in the *Revue blanche*, 1st sem. 1897, p. 157.

poems—*Les Vierges se mirent dans les miroirs*—seem to be inspired by *The Lady of Shalott*:[1]

> A nos fenêtres, à nos miroirs,
> Le soleil agonise en baisers de lumière
> Et là-bas l'orbe large embrasse la clairière
> De la forêt obscure vers la Ville et la Mer.
> Déjà d'étranges visions ce soir
> Glissent pâles aux vitraux lourds de nos fenêtres
> Et se meurent en l'or de nos miroirs.
> Chevauchées
> Vers quelle destinée? ô Rois! et quels espoirs
> Vous guident par la nuit vers nos ternes miroirs
> Où les éclairs de vos cimiers se meurent?
> . . . .
> En vain de nos fenêtres
> Vers vous que nous rêvions les Rois de notre espoir
> Nous fîmes au crépuscule un geste d'espoir.
> O fantômes de nos miroirs
> Fantômes déjà du passé
> Nos yeux vous ont guettés sous l'or de nos miroirs
> Aux baisers apeurés des mouvantes lumières
> Jusqu'au rêve reflété de la clairière
> Dans l'or de nos miroirs ou d'antiques fenêtres.
> Vous n'étiez pas un rêve vide
> O vous qui chevauchez parmi les fleurs lointaines
> Vers la promesse de mes lèvres avides:
> . . . .
> Vos formes n'étaient pas d'un mensonger nuage
> Qu'un songe seul douait de vie ou d'un visage,
> Vous êtes les Chevaliers tard-venus
> Que m'annoncèrent dans la fièvre du jeune âge
> Les signes certains de magiques présages. . . .

[1] In an article on Rossetti in the *M. de F.*, May 16, 1908, Fontainas speaks of Tennyson as "a wonderfully balanced and delicate artist". The same poem seems to have suggested the poem *Élise aux Fusées* in *Filles-fleurs* (Paris, *M. de F.*, 1895), by Tristan Klingsor, who also writes of a Lady Elaine, of Iseult, and of Myrdhinn. He too has a fondness for the word 'samite'.

Attracted by chivalric legends, and having Celtic blood in his veins, the poet Louis le Cardonnel loved the "legendary grace" of Tennyson. Le Cardonnel, who would have the poet be a prophet, is drawn, too, by the nobility and purity of Tennyson's poetry. As Le Cardonnel's call to a religious life becomes more and more definite, his poetry bears more and more the mark of his mystic faith and his love of the Holy City, but the influence of Tennyson is evident in his early poems, in the very conception of his poetry, in the music of the whole. This resemblance struck Édouard Schuré, who in 1902, hearing for the first time in the *salon* of Madame Gabrielle Delzant *Vallis Amantium* and other poems of Louis le Cardonnel, exclaimed: "Why is it that this French Tennyson is still unknown"?[1] Le Cardonnel's song is less varied than that of Tennyson, but it has a similar full, smooth harmony, in which sound and sense are united by skilful exploitation of the resources of alliteration and assonance. Le Cardonnel has Tennyson's reticence: the same quiet melancholy: the figures of his dreams move in the same land of magic and legend. Love in his poetry is chaste and wistful, bringing with it longings for the unseen, and

> Tendresses dont l'ardeur s'enveloppe de songe.[2]

Like Tennyson he loves the sea, great spaces, flying white clouds, and starry skies. Thus he sings of his great hero, his poet:

> Il chérit la mer et l'aventure,
> Il veut devant lui l'espace ouvert,
> Du regard il boit le ciel entier;

---

[1] Édouard Schuré, *Femmes inspiratrices et poètes annonciateurs*, Paris: Perrin, 1908, in-16, p. 318.
[2] *Poèmes* (M. de F., 1904): *Vallis Amantium*.

TENNYSON AND SYMBOLIST MOVEMENT

> Pour compagne il prend la Solitude
> Et le vent sauvage est son ami.
> (*Poèmes*: *Le Tailleur de Tombes*.)

In praise of Tennyson he wrote one of his finest poems, here quoted in part:

> Fleurs de mélancolie et fleurs de piété,
> Tombez sur Tennyson, qui nous charma les heures,
> Sur Tennyson aux chants si limpidement beaux,
> Qu'à jamais leur cadence enchante nos demeures
> Et que nos cœurs lui sont palais plus que tombeaux,
> Tombez sur Tennyson, le délivré des heures.
>
> . . . . . .
>
> Le don mystérieux d'éveiller l'Infini,
> Nous l'avons, comme toi, de par nos aïeux celtes,
> Et le songe n'est pas de nos fronts si banni
> Que sur ton vaisseau blanc peuplé de vierges sveltes
> Nous ne puissions te suivre au pays de l'Infini.
>
> . . . . . .
>
> Bruits des pas du printemps qui vient par les vallons,
> Frissons de la forêt magiquement profonde,
> Où Viviane encore peigne ses cheveux blonds,
> Murmure, dans le soir, des voix de l'autre monde,
> Frémissements de sources en de secrets vallons.
>
> Et nous qui souhaitons que divinement claire,
> La poésie enfin retrouve son azur,
> Nous adorons surtout ta grâce légendaire,
> O Tennyson, cor d'ivoire dans le soir pur,
> O Tennyson, cloche d'argent dans l'aube claire.
> (*Poèmes*, p. 73: *La Louange de Tennyson*.)[1]

Such are the poets who, forsaking the outworn Parnassian tradition, kept within them, as they groped their way towards a less circumscribed poetic domain, some memory of the ample symbolism of the Arthurian legend.

[1] First published in *La Revue hebdomadaire*, Sept. 1893.

If, after a time, this mode of legendary mysticism produced an overabundance of Thules and Avalons, of pale ladies and allegorical knights fighting monsters known only to heraldry, we owe to it also such poems as Verlaine's *Parsifal* and his *Bon chevalier masqué qui chevauche en silence*. In all its manifestations, even the most absurd, this new fashion for chivalry had merit as an endeavour to throw off the tyranny of a materialism which had become intolerable, and to seek adventure in lands of the imagination.

CHAPTER VII

REVIEW AND READJUSTMENT

I. *Tennyson's Death*

TENNYSON's death in 1892 set the stream of criticism flowing afresh. Articles of all kinds, some betraying a perfunctory, others a very real interest in their subject, give us a sort of crystallisation of opinions held upon Tennyson in all circles in France. The newspapers hasten to offer their views: " *L'incompétence de même compte: et la grande presse ou quotidienne ici manifeste un peu la sienne, autrement que par une louable pudeur,*" remarked Mallarmé.[1]

Hence we find hasty judgments in which the writers hardly trouble to conceal their irritation or boredom. The most widespread and comprehensible mistake is that of seeing in Tennyson only the official poet.[2] A journalist of the *Écho de Paris*, although fresh from an interview with the fervent *anglicisant* James Darmesteter, discusses ironically the choice of a new Laureate.[3] "The Queen of England possesses gentlemen-in-ordinary, officers, maids of honour, chambermaids, and scullions. She has also

---

[1] *Divagations* (Paris: Fasquelle, 1897): *Tennyson vu d'ici*. This article first appeared in the *National Observer*, Oct. 24, 1892; it was reprinted in the *Revue blanche*, Dec. 1892, and quoted by the *M. de F.* vol. vii. 1893.

[2] Better-known critics went no deeper than this. Jules Lemaître, criticising certain aspects of Virgil's poetry, says: "He was an official poet, a laureate, a Tennyson" (*Les Contemporains*, 6th series: *Figurines*, p. 277).

[3] G. Steigler, *Écho de Paris*, Oct. 18, 1892.

her poet. Forty years of funeral laments and epithalamia, of official tears and laughter, what a task!" Who claims this thankless heritage? *"A vos luths, messieurs les poètes, c'est Sa Majesté qui donne le la."* A further tendency was to look on Tennyson solely as a poet for the vicarage or the girls' school—as the women's poet—worse, as the Englishwoman's poet. In the *Figaro* of October 7, one Jacques Saint-Cère, endeavouring to live up to his pseudonym, expresses his scorn for the chromo-lithographic poems of this English Cabanel who "answered to the liking for home, tea, and ethereal poetry which dwells in the bosom of every Englishwoman over forty". He affirms that "poetry, perhaps, may not suffer excessively from his passing". F. Loliée, in the *Nouvelle Revue* of November 1892, describes him as a poet to ravish *"l'imagination des sensibles ladies"*. André Theuriet, writing in *Le Journal* (October 17, 1892), compares him with Octave Feuillet, basing his analogy on the charm which both writers had over the feminine mind, a charm which, according to Theuriet, was deliberate and calculated. Here comes a pleasant example of the vagaries of criticism: after making this unflattering comparison, Theuriet can hardly have been overjoyed to read the statement by C. Looten in the *Revue de Lille* that, among all his French contemporaries, the one who shows closest kinship with Tennyson is the poet and novelist André Theuriet.[1]

More generous critics claim a share of England's sorrow. "We too shall keep within us", writes Augustin Filon in the *Journal des Débats* of October 11, "something gained from Tennyson which has become part of our moral being." "The whole civilised world will mourn in him one of its most charming, most harmonious, and

[1] See four long articles in the *Revue de Lille*, Jan.-April 1893.

tenderest singers", writes the critic of the *Gaulois*;[1] "he went beyond the insular bounds of his native country, and succeeded in giving to his songs that immortal charm which characterises the Homeric poems and the ballads of the Middle Ages." F. de P. in the *Temps* (October 7) protests against the fashionable disparagement of Tennyson, in which he sees the influence of Taine. He grants that Tennyson saw life and humanity "*sous un rayon un peu trop gris-perle*", but he defends him against the charge of effeminate aestheticism which average opinion in France brings against him. In the *Idylls*, for example, "he was worthy to be associated, where an entire part of his inspiration was concerned, with the Wagner of Tristan and Isolde and Parsifal. . . . Generous inspiration, preoccupation with the problems of his day, expectation and desire of a freer and wider future, meditation, often full of distress, on the conquests of reason and conscience in the domain of personal religion, none of these things was lacking in him, and it is just because he poured that somewhat dark and troubled liquor—the only liquor that can slake the thirst of our modern souls—into a delicately chased cup of exquisite workmanship and of precious metal—for that very reason he was not only an artist for drawing-rooms and schoolrooms, but a great and true poet, the last of the line of Spenser."

These more responsible critics are by no means unconscious of the limits of Tennyson's genius. They take him at his true value and see in him an exquisite singer and a man of sincerity. That is enough for them. "He gave the world music and images and not doctrines", writes Augustin Filon.[2] Madame Darmesteter, who, as

[1] De Blowitz, Oct. 7, 1892.
[2] *Journal des Débats*, Oct. 11, 1892.

Mary Robinson, had written poetry not free from Tennyson's influence, pleads his cause in the *Revue bleue* of November 11. For her, Tennyson is purely a lyric poet, "one of those aerial creatures who are a divine voice and nothing more. He thought well and with sincerity, but he thought little, and his thoughts were at the mercy of his feelings. He was a poet, and nothing but a poet." This idea was developed in a delightful article in the *Figaro*[3] by Téodor de Wyzéwa, a critic downright and self-willed in his judgments who acknowledged only three contemporary English writers—Tennyson, Morris, and Froude—as really remarkable. He refers to the Laureate, loved by the lettered and the ignorant alike, as the *"Grand dispensateur national du rêve et de la poésie"*. He considers that one of the qualities which made Tennyson a magnificent poet was his complete lack of intelligence; "it was not", he adds, "an argumentative sort of unintelligence, such as so many poets possess, but simply a complete incapacity to think for himself. . . . His general ideas were lamentably poor. On problems of art, philosophy, politics, he always kept to the most ordinary of commonplaces." From this point of view he compares him favourably with Browning. Thus Tennyson was above all the poet of emotions, of sentiments, of gentle or violent passions. To these sentiments he gave a form that was "almost too perfect, too pure, and too noble to respond as yet to the genius of his race: it was a quasi-Virgilian form, so discreet in its varying tones that it has often prevented people from realising the heat and intensity of the feeling contained in it." His work is the most perfect artistic product of the English nineteenth century.

[1] Oct. 9, 1892, reprinted in the first series of *Écrivains étrangers* (Paris: Perrin, 1896).

In an interview published by the *Écho de Paris* Mallarmé declared that France had been supremely unjust to Tennyson.[1] "Tennyson had an ardent nature devoted to an art at once melancholy and violent, calm and impetuous, in turn elegant and susceptible, passionate and proud: his stanzas might be highly coloured, or of penetrating sadness." It is doubtful whether this interviewer is quite to be trusted, for he makes Mallarmé say, in comparing Tennyson with Puvis de Chavannes, that the *serene beauty* of *Maud* equals that of the Pantheon frescoes.

Happily, we have at first hand in *Divagations* a characteristic summing-up by Mallarmé of the French attitude towards Tennyson, in which Mallarmé is not sparing in his praise. He regrets that he has not been able to consult other French poets—"who, cloistered within their own opinions or faithful to the language whose instinct they exalt, are loath, as it were, to admit any other: under that aspect they remain, to a greater degree than anybody else, patriotic". The reading public takes little interest in Tennyson: "it calls to mind a monumental passage by Taine on the mature Alfred Tennyson, but hardly refers at all to sources". *Enoch Arden* has become a school-book. As for the *Idylls*, "the fashion, contemporary with Gustave Doré, about twenty years ago, laid on drawing-room tables a luxuriously bound folio volume closed on a version of several of the *Idylls*", left to grow musty in their elegant surroundings.

Mallarmé, the morbidly sensitive artist who was so merciless a critic of his own work, utters his amazement at the perfection and the range of Tennyson's poetry, from the first poems down to *Demeter*. His own preferences are for *Maud*, "*romantique, moderne, et songes et passion*",

[1] Oct. 8, 1892: Ch. Fromentin, *Tennyson chez Stéphane Mallarmé.*

which is yet not so characteristic of Tennyson as *"ce récité toujours ou murmuré* Locksley Hall, *ou tels enchantements que* The Lotos-Eaters, Oenone; *ou* In Memoriam, *cimetière pour un mort seul"*.

Mallarmé does not hesitate to affirm that Tennyson is destined to become better and better understood in France. By a typical artifice he interprets the sentiments provoked by "that chaste sequence of syllables—Tennyson. I know that already it summons up and arouses, and will do so more and more, in spite even of the misunderstanding between one language and another, in spite of gaps and lack of comprehension—the thought of an august and tender figure, strong of will, simple, and taciturn; and I would almost add that his calm death confers a sort of loneliness on it, and completes for the world its proud seclusion."

Frankly, with affection and respect, Mallarmé pays his tribute to Tennyson. "Everything which literary culture carried with certainty, originality, and good taste to a superior plane, that of art, added to a fundamental and exquisite poetic gift, can produce in an exceptional man, Tennyson had at his command, without ever losing hold on it, throughout the disquieting variety of his work. To have enriched the voice with intonations not previously heard (and certainly but for Tennyson a music characteristic of him would be missing in English as I sing it), and to have made the national poetical instrument yield certain new but admittedly innate chords, constitutes the poet, in the full measure of his task and of his prestige."

The writer of these words set such a value on poetic inspiration and perfection of form that in the end he chose to be silent rather than fall short of his own ideal. His was praise not lightly given.

Several reviews paid their homage to Tennyson by translating some of his poems. *La Plume* for November 1892 publishes a translation of *The Poet* by Henri Bérenger (p. 466). Olivier-Georges Destrée in the *Revue générale* gives admirable translations of *Oenone* and *The Merman* (December 1892, p. 872). *La Revue hebdomadaire* gives translations of *Come into the Garden, Maud, The Deserted House, The Death of the Old Year,* by Félix Jeantet. Louis le Cardonnel's *Louange d'Alfred Tennyson* also appears in the *Revue hebdomadaire* (September 1893, pp. 292-296). *Le Mercure de France* publishes in November 1892 four sonnets by Jean Lorrain in the manner of Tennyson's *Idylls of the King*—*Énide, Viviane, Élaine, Genièvre*: they are like four windows in a chapel, or four panels by Burne-Jones. Here is the sonnet *Élaine*:

> L'allée est droite, obscure et pleine de pervenches.
> Dans le corsage étroit d'une robe à longs plis
> Et les deux bras chargés de lys qu'elle a cueillis
> La svelte et pure Élaine apparaît dans les branches.
>
> Un essaim de ramiers rôde autour de ses hanches,
> Blanc essor attiré par la blancheur des lys;
> Au loin, sur l'or rose d'un ciel aux tons palis,
> Le manoir d'Astolat et ses tourelles blanches.
>
> Élaine aux yeux d'aurore, au rire humide et frais,
> A sa place marquée aux jardins de cyprès;
> Élaine avec les lys sera morte à l'automne.
>
> Élaine est destinée aux éternels regrets,
> Et présageant l'ennui d'une fin monotone,
> Pâle et froide à ses pieds fleurit une anémone.

II. *Biographies*

From this point we might expect to discover a steady waning of the interest which Tennyson had provoked during his lifetime. But Mallarmé's prophecy, in surprising measure, came true. First the *Memoir* of Hallam Lord Tennyson, published in 1897, again turned public attention upon the poet. The book said nothing very new about Tennyson: it amplified facts more or less known already. Yet it gave a more intimate view of the poet: though still idealised, he was here to be studied as a human being, with his humours and his oddnesses. This study offered, in a most unattractive form, a mass of facts and anecdotes grouped with no regard for other than chronological order: in France it provided material for at least eight voluminous articles, of which two appeared later in book form.[1]

Whilst finding much interesting matter in these memoirs, critics made severe comments on the slovenly method of arrangement. Victor Cherbuliez, in the opening sentences of a lively article, observes that the poet had not bequeathed to his son his hatred of long-windedness and irrelevant detail. H. D. Davray resents Hallam Lord Tennyson's constant effort to surround his father with a halo, and considers the second volume, with its "flood of pompous letters", altogether wearisome. Yet each man took the trouble to digest these two large volumes and to give his own interpretation of them.

These interpretations are pleasantly varied. One article works the poet's life into a touching story for the *Revue des Jeunes Filles* (three of Tennyson's poems had already provided stories for the innocuous *Bibliothèque rose*). Another article is interested chiefly in his intellectual life and literary relations. A third attempts a discussion of his

---

[1] Viz. Père Ragey, *Tennyson*, Paris (Delhomme et Briguet), 1899, 409 pp., first published serially in *L'Université catholique de Lyon*. C. Looten, *Une Biographie de Tennyson*, Arras (Sueur-Charruey), 1900, 23 pp., first appeared in the *Revue de Lille*. For the other six articles see Bibliography, p. 159.

religious faith. All have this in common, that they put Tennyson within every man's reach.

The Révérend Père Ragey undertook to rewrite the biography. His aim was to sort out the mass of facts and to preserve all that might interest a French public, and thus to produce a complete and coherent study. The work was necessary and the intention praiseworthy. The result was less admirable than the intention. The reverend Father was a fervent admirer of Tennyson. His only complaint against him was that, not being a Catholic, he was only half a Christian. At times he makes use of Tennyson's lofty morality in order to attack the diabolical cynicism and profanity of the followers of Byron or the realist school. At other times he withdraws from this alliance in order to deplore Tennyson's protestantism, which, in his opinion, prevents the poet's work from achieving full artistic perfection. How much more interesting, and generally picturesque, he observes, would Annie of *Enoch Arden* have been had she knelt before a picture of the Virgin above her bed, instead of merely seeking a sign in her Bible.

The fact was that Father Ragey had not, any more than the second Lord Tennyson, the critical spirit needed in a biographer. He did not go deep enough; he never really grappled with his subject. Despite his intention of abridging he quotes in and out of season Victor Hugo, Lamartine, de Musset, and Sainte-Beuve. He interlards a study of Tennyson's life with analyses and long dissertations on his work. Abbé Brémond counts this study as one of the *"belles audaces"* of Father Ragey, one of the big subjects which "he assaults with a kind of impatient ardour". He thanks him, somewhat evasively, for having attempted what so many others, "after being moved by the immortal stanzas of *In Memoriam* or after meditating on the sublime words of the dying Arthur", have promised themselves to do, and have never done for fear of not loving and understanding enough this noble poetry.[1]

This book of Père Ragey's did fill a gap, and it had the great quality of sincerity. Moreover it brought into prominence facts too readily overlooked when people discussed the Laureate, with his wealth, honours, and popularity—it recalled the disappointments of the early years, the severity of critics, the neurasthenic depression against which he struggled for years and which was only dispelled by constant intellectual effort. This biography enabled C. Looten to write his study of Tennyson, a small but admirably concise essay which, less ambitious than the work that inspired it, shows a far keener critical sense, and a much closer understanding of the subject.

III. *Translations*

By making known Tennyson's life and thought, these studies prepared the way for the most ambitious translations of his work that have appeared in France—those by Léon Morel.[2] To translate *In Memoriam* into French verse was a task demanding, besides very sure taste and poetic feeling, rare courage and patience. Léon Morel had all these qualities.

He admired *In Memoriam* profoundly, and tried to give through his version some glimpse of its austere splendour. His translation is scrupulously exact. In his

---

[1] See in *Études religieuses, historiques et littéraires*, No. 81, 1899, pp. 376-378.
[2] *In Memoriam*, traduit en vers français par Léon Morel, Paris (Hachette), 1898 (2nd edition, Hachette, 1899). *Poèmes divers d'Alfred Tennyson*, traduits en vers français par Léon Morel, Paris (Hachette), 1899.

verse he keeps the original arrangement of the rimes, and follows, with astonishing ingenuity, the very cadences of Tennyson's English. Errors of interpretation are entirely absent. With admirable tact and certainty he renders the most obscure and abstract passages, as in this strophe where Tennyson's concision itself tells against the clear expression of his thought:

> Oh, if indeed that eye foresee
>   Or see (in Him is no before)
>   In more of life true life no more
> And Love the indifference to be . . .
> <div align="right">(<i>In Memoriam</i>, xxvi.)</div>

> Ah, si réellement ce regard doit prévoir
> Ou voir (puisque pour Lui le temps est sans époque)
> En ma vie à venir un regret équivoque
> Si le matin Amour, elle doit être au soir
>
> Indifférence . . .

At times his translation lacks, through its sheer fidelity, the appearance of a French poem. The rimes are, of necessity, somewhat laboured, but the phrasing is rarely commonplace, and is often happy, as, for example, in the bell-like effect which he makes by the alternation of the sounds *onne* and *elle* in *Ring out, wild bells*, the full resonance of which, as Morel himself observes, no translation can reproduce:

> Sonne pour elle un glas, sonne pour la nouvelle,
> Sonne, cloche joyeuse, au dessus du sol blanc:
> Un an s'enfuit: suis-le de ton adieu tremblant,
> Sonne le glas du faux, et que ta voix appelle
> Le seul vrai . . .

The whole work is worthy of *In Memoriam*, and was much appreciated. Augustin Filon, in the *Journal des*

Débats,[1] gives it warm praise, seeing in it a masterpiece of patience, taste, and feeling; he points out that, to attain the concision of the English, Morel has made use of monosyllables with a boldness and a success that would not have been thought possible in French. "His book is a novel and interesting piece of work, and at the same time one of the finest examples one could give of the desperate and successful struggle of a translator with his original, of one poet with another." M. Lanson[2] is amazed at the ingenuity and resource which were needed in order to follow the original so closely in verse which is almost everywhere easy and natural; believing as he does that a translation into verse is a double treachery, he yet considers that nothing better than this version will ever be done. A second edition appeared in 1909.[3]

Tennyson's poem probably inspired certain *In Memoriams* which were published after 1850. At least two can be related to it, one of which interests us inasmuch as it comes from the poet-critic who in 1872 affected to despise "*le miel et le lait du trop doux Tennyson*".[4] Later, in his despair at the loss of his child, Émile Blémont remembered lines of Tennyson which had moved him:

> Par la nuit morne, au bruit du vent,
> Dans mon esprit passe souvent
> Quatre beaux vers doux et funèbres . . .
> Lus aux jours où je m'aveuglais

---

[1] Jan. 25, 1899: *L'Art de traduire*. Abbé Brémond also praises this translation in the article in the *Études* quoted above.

[2] *Revue universitaire*, 1898, 2nd sem. p. 485.

[3] Six of the poems of this translation were set to music by Max d'Ollone (Paris, Heugel, 1910).

[4] In an article on Swinburne in *La Renaissance*, April 27, 1872: see also his article on Tennyson quoted above. Blémont's poem *En Mémoire d'un enfant* was published in 1899 (Paris, Lemerre). The other *In Memoriam* is by Eugène Aubert: *Élans et tristesses* (Paris, 1884), a series of mediocre poems which includes a pastiche of *Ring out, wild bells*.

De poésie et de chimère
Afin d'aimer la vie amère.

A les lire, sur le moment,
J'eus un obscur pressentiment
De quelque tristesse mortelle.
On y parle, je me rappelle,

D'un enfant pleurant dans la nuit,
Pleurant dans l'ombre où rien ne luit,
Et n'ayant, hélas! d'autres armes
Contre la douleur, que les larmes.

En mémoire d'un enfant, a series of forty short poems, follows the stages of his grief. It has been called a miniature *In Memoriam*.[1]

This image of the child crying in the night may have suggested to Charles Guérin, who read Tennyson, the image which he uses more than once in *Le Cœur solitaire*:

Hélas! ô vœux d'enfant craintif perdu dans l'ombre.
(p. 123.)

On a des mots d'enfant qui pleurent et supplient
Vers ce vaste univers qu'on voudrait croire Dieu.[2]
(p. 39.)

---

[1] H. Potez, *Les Poètes des morts* (*Manuel gén. de l'Instruction primaire*, Oct. 26, 1899).

[2] See *Le Cœur solitaire* (*Mercure de France*), 1898, xlvi. p. 123; *Fenêtres sur la vie*, xiii. p. 39, vii. p. 21. It would be absurd to attribute to Tennyson that autumnal sadness which is in Guérin, but it would seem that the following poem would not have had quite the same form if Tennyson had not written *Tears, idle tears*:

". . . Connaissez-vous ma peine,
La peine que je porte au fond de l'âme? Elle est
Pâle comme un soleil déclinant sur la vigne,
Fraîche comme le grès d'une jarre de lait,
Et frémissant aussi comme un duvet de cygne,
Peine qu'on ne saurait nommer, chagrin sans cause

Morel, encouraged by assurances from various readers that his *In Memoriam* had introduced to them a poet whom they had hitherto known only by name, undertook to translate a selection of Tennyson's poems, wishing to show this time, as he says in his preface, "how rich, supple, and fertile the master's genius was". By a skilful choice he shows Tennyson in all his aspects, from the first ballads down to *The Silent Voices* and *Crossing the Bar*, from the tranquil idylls down to *Rizpah*. Reluctantly he detaches from the *Idylls* and *The Princess* (poems too long to fit his restricted framework) the lyric pieces which form their greatest charm and of which he gives delightful translations.

Léon Morel here set himself a task even more delicate than that of translating *In Memoriam*. In his preface he compares himself to an engraver who transposes a painting into another and less rich form of art. "No doubt", he says, "he is doomed beforehand to give but an imperfect reproduction of his model, but he can and must set out to fix in his translation the impression he has received. If his engraving succeeds in conveying that impression to others, although with less clearness and intensity, he has been a useful and faithful interpreter."

Here the translator was faced with a formidable variety of rhythms and harmonies. Here again he often had to deal with poems of a musical rather than a logical

> D'orphelin qu'à la nuit nulle chanson ne berce. . . .
> Cette peine est vraiment trop obscure ce soir."
> (p. 46.)

Elsewhere (p. 47) he speaks of a September evening "si doux qu'on en voudrait pleurer"; and on p. 57

> "D'autres viendront pareils à moi dans leur chair veuve
> Le cœur amer d'un vieil amour encore vivace,
> Voir parmi les corbeaux qui volent vers sa face
> Le soleil se coucher sur *des moissons heureuses*."

REVIEW AND READJUSTMENT

unity. But he displays remarkable accuracy and resourcefulness. This example, from *Oenone*, one of the most charming of interpretations, shows how he follows the fine rhythm of Tennyson:

> He smiled, and opening out his milk-white palm,
> Disclosed a fruit of pure Hesperian gold,
> That smelt ambrosially, and while I looked
> And listened, the full-flowing river of speech
> Came down upon my heart.
> My own Oenone. . . .

> Souriant il ouvrait sa main blanche et nacrée
> Et me fit voir un fruit à l'écorce dorée
> Au parfum d'ambroisie; et moi, le regardant,
> J'écoutais: sa parole en un flot abondant
> Inondait tout mon cœur.
> O mon aimée Oenone. . . .

This is only one example of the method which he uses throughout, generally with perfect success.

Inevitably there is not the same degree of merit in all these translations. The lyric poems, divested of their musical value, of the associations conveyed by the word, lose much of their charm.

> To throng with stately blooms the breathing spring
>   Of Hope and Youth
> (*The Poet*)

does not live again in

> Pour enrichir des fleurs d'espoir le printemps
>   De nos jeunes années.

Nor did Morel always succeed in keeping the distinction of Tennyson's images, as may be seen from this example in *Locksley Hall*:

> Woman is the lesser man, and all thy passions, matched with mine,
> Are as moonlight unto sunlight, and as water unto wine.

> La femme est un homme plus faible: pour nos cœurs
> Il n'est pas de mesure commune;
> Au vin compare-t-on l'eau froide et sans saveurs
> Au chaud soleil le clair de lune?

Yet on the whole Morel accomplished admirably a somewhat thankless task. His translations do honour to Tennyson.

How much more laborious and thankless was the enterprise of Édouard Rastoul, who between 1907 and 1908 published translations of three of Tennyson's dramas —*The Falcon*, *Becket*, and *Queen Mary*—without either preface or notes. This was a curious form of devotion, but whether to Tennyson or the Drama one cannot say.[1]

IV. *Centenary Opinions*

Centenary judgments on a poet are not particularly trustworthy. On the one hand, the centenary, being an opportunity to honour his memory, calls for eulogies which are not always discreet; as, on the other hand, it often falls in the midst of the reaction against the poet's artistic and other beliefs, it is often the signal for outbursts of irritation. The mean term of these two extremes in criticism may be difficult to find.

This was so in England at the time of Tennyson's centenary. Tennyson represented the Victorian era, with all its limitations, illusions, and enthusiasms. In 1909 his work had not yet taken on the charm of antiquity. It was out of date, being of yesterday. Voices in his defence were, of course, not lacking. Sir Herbert Warren in his

---

[1] *Le Faucon*, saynète en un acte traduite et mise en vers par É. Rastoul, Avignon (F. Seguin, 1907). *Thomas Becket*, traduit et mis en vers par É. Rastoul (*id.*, 1907). *Marie Tudor*, traduit et mis en vers par É. Rastoul (*id.*, 1908).

memorial lecture at Oxford pointed out that for a long time he had been in advance of the thought of his age, that he had always tried to keep abreast of it, and that only towards the end of his life had he dropped behind. It was chiefly the social and intellectual progress achieved since his death that made Tennyson's thought seem out of date. W. P. Ker, speaking at Cambridge, showed that the true, and noblest, thought of Tennyson was to be found, not in the discursive poems but in the antique and legendary poems where he expresses himself through symbols.[1]

Nevertheless the reaction against Tennyson in England was marked. In France the centenary was the occasion of a new series of articles which attempted to pass final judgment on the poet. It may be that French criticism tried to show generosity to the foreigner; or it may be that since among impartial critics admiration had never been exaggerated, the reaction was less violent. It is certain that these centenary articles show no disparagement of Tennyson.[2] The critics who follow most closely the literary movements among their neighbours—those of the *Mercure de France*, the *Temps*, which quotes Edmund

---

[1] See *The Centenary of Tennyson*, Oxford (Clarendon Press), 1909, and *Tennyson* (Cambridge University Press), 1909.
[2] See *L'Écho de Paris*, Aug. 6, Edmond Pilon: *Alfred Tennyson*.
Journal des Débats, Sept. 29, A. Filon: *Le Centenaire de Tennyson à Oxford*.
Le Temps, Aug. 11, anon.: *Le Centenaire de Tennyson*.
Mercure de France, Aug. 16, H. D. Davray: *Alfred Tennyson*.
Quarterly Review, April, E. Faguet: *The Centenary of Tennyson*.
Revue bleue, Aug. 21, Jacques Lux: *Le Centenaire de Tennyson*.
R. D. M., Aug. 5, Firmin Roz: *Tennyson*.
L'Opinion, Aug. 7, Georges Grappe: *Alfred Tennyson*.
Le Correspondant, July 25, Abbé Brémond: *Le Centenaire de Tennyson*.
La Revue hebdomadaire, Sept.: *Poèmes d'Alfred Tennyson*, translated with comments by Firmin Roz.

In *Le Gaulois* of Aug. 10 is a curious note on the love of France for the great poet Tennyson, and the love of the great poet Tennyson for France.

Gosse, the *Revue bleue*, which quotes the *Quarterly* and the *Nation*—are satisfied with stating that Tennyson's glory will inevitably suffer some eclipse, but do not go too deeply into the question. Other critics, like Émile Faguet, Augustin Filon, Firmin Roz, Edmond Pilon, without blinding themselves to Tennyson's faults, declare that the world is the richer for his noble verse and his noble life, and that in this perfectly wrought poetry there is a lofty and magnanimous soul that time will not harm.

"The object here is to understand Tennyson's greatness: his weaknesses do not explain that." So writes M. Firmin Roz, who traces the intellectual and artistic development of the poet in an acute and delicate study which may be regarded as a standard work.[1] These critics, however they differ, saw through Tennyson's reserve and found not only the serene, confident artist, but also the man who, having suffered, mastered his sorrows and left only the reflection of them in his work. Faguet declares that Tennyson had in him all the qualities of a morbid, passionate poet; but he had no desire to make literature of that sort. For Faguet, the essential unity of Tennyson's work consists in his fervent, unfaltering love of beauty. He sings the beauty of sorrow as if the soul of his friend lived and spoke within him. Tennyson's instinct for beauty is well represented in the figures of his women, touching and melancholy, slightly veiled or seen vaguely through hovering mist. "His muse resembles a beautiful woman, mourning and only half-consoled." F. Roz notes his fondness for dim, mysterious words; his songs are "the pure music of a sad and sensitive soul, the most lovely music that English words have ever formed".

[1] Reprinted in the series *Les Grands Écrivains étrangers* (Bloud, 1911).

These critics are unanimous in deploring Taine's injustice towards Tennyson. "What causes this impression of monotony and implacable beauty in Alfred Tennyson", says Edmond Pilon, "is never anything but a sentiment of modesty, of admirable reticence. But in reality a secret fire burns beneath these light, shining ashes, and a soul dwells in the depths of these legends." Similarly M. Firmin Roz says: "Though in the first place Tennyson was outwardly the most delicate, exquisite, and fastidious of artists, he expressed none the less, in all their richness and complexity, the spirit of his time and the soul of his race, along with something that was still more profound, universal, and lasting: I mean the eternal poetry of humanity, in its purest, if not in its most intense form."

Though Faguet considered Tennyson's patriotic poetry stiff and insincere, more than one of his colleagues succeeded in admiring the tact and feeling with which the poet accomplished his task of interpreting national sentiment. Firmin Roz translated the *Ode on the Death of the Duke of Wellington,* and thought that not enough importance had been given in France to Tennyson's official poetry. Georges Grappe also stresses Tennyson's national inspiration: "His soul, far better than Hugo's, to whom he has often been compared, resounded and vibrated with all the emotions of his nation; for, rising above party, he succeeded in divesting himself of hatred, in being all love." The inaccuracy of the latter part of the remark is only apparent, for in comparison with Hugo's vituperation of Napoleon III., Tennyson's comments on the Manchester school were mere friendly criticism.

But while critics laid emphasis on his relationship to his country and his age, all saw in him a poet for humanity and not for one nation alone. "This work, as English as Kipling's," writes M. Firmin Roz, "has nevertheless a universal, a human value. Tennyson's poetry, by its sympathy, reaches those depths of the spiritual life where local and special differences cease to exist. We should all lose by not hearing the Tennysonian music which charmed England. He was a great poet, both of his country and of humanity. For his country and for the world it is better that he should have lived." And Faguet: "He is one of those who honour, not only the country in which he was born and the language in which he wrote, but humanity at large". These riper judgments show a great respect for Tennyson. Impartially the tale of his qualities and faults has been told, and the memory that remains is that of a great and noble figure.[1]

---

[1] After the centenary articles, few articles dealing solely with Tennyson are found. See, however, *Alfred Tennyson, le poète-lauréat*, by Ernest Dupuy, *Rev. hebdomadaire*, Jan. 1915.

CONCLUSION

How far was Tennyson really known in France? In following the fortunes of his work among the French critics we have found a marked development of sympathy and understanding. Such a progress is no doubt natural, but would not have been maintained had it not been provoked by genuine interest.

In the beginning, while the echoes of romantic lyricism still lingered, the impersonal note in his poetry was misunderstood: it was explained by calling him a metaphysical poet. The great critics of the middle of the century appreciated him better, but saw only the artist and dilettante. The next generation discovered idealism in him, as well as social and humanitarian preoccupations. When, later still, it was seen that those beliefs and ideals of his were characteristic of the Victorian era then drawing to its close, people admired or disliked Tennyson as they disliked or admired his age. The critics who wrote on the centenary, looking back over the nineteenth century, inclined to indulgence: whereas for the twentieth-century critics his work is the symbol of a spiritual despotism. "In Tennyson", writes M. Valéry Larbaud,[1] "I am too conscious of the poet of one period, and, to be frank, of one class, a class whose teaching methods, whose ideas

---

[1] M. Larbaud is here establishing a contrast between Tennyson and Patmore, to Patmore's advantage. See in the *Nouvelle Revue française* (Sept. 1 and Oct. 1, 1911) the article by M. Larbaud which serves as introduction to poems of Patmore adapted by Paul Claudel.

and aspirations, tyrannised over my youth and for long kept my mind in grievous bondage. I feel too strongly that he was the poet of the *bourgeoisie*. I hate his vague deism, his Darwinism, his chauvinism, his absurd belief in progress." If we leave out those parts of his work which are already time-worn, and grant that this "widest-known retailer of ideas in English verse"[1] comes off badly if examined solely from the intellectual point of view, there still remain his exquisite lyric gift and his august personality. The beauty of form in Tennyson's work was fully appreciated in France. Not one critic, in a country which sets such value on formal beauty, and appraises it with such supreme skill, omits his tribute to Tennyson as an artist. Some critics even held that poems like *Enoch Arden*, being products of a subtle and effortless art, have been more completely admired in France than in England; on the occasion of the centenary, one critic, certainly no partisan of Tennyson, since he ranked him as "a kind of François Coppée for the well-to-do", affirmed that for perfection of form Milton is the only poet to whom Tennyson can be compared.[2]

Sir Herbert Warren, in his centenary lecture on Tennyson at Oxford, gave his opinion that, except Shakespeare, and in some respects Byron, no English poet has been more universally known than Tennyson. He alludes to his success in Germany,[3] where after 1842 he was repeatedly translated, and to France, that "land of distin-

[1] Mr. Oliver Elton in a lecture on Tennyson at Liverpool in 1901.
[2] H. D. Davray in the article already quoted.
[3] Knowledge of Tennyson's work spread more rapidly in Germany than in France. F. Freiligrath translated poems in 1842: two volumes of translations appeared in 1853 (*Gedichte*, W. Hertzberg; *Ausgewählte Gedichte*, H. Fischer). A translation of *In Memoriam* by W. Hertzberg appeared in 1854. Subsequent translations are more numerous than in France.

guished and distinguishing criticism", where his work has been the subject of a continuous series of reviews and studies. Does that series of studies mean that Tennyson's work now belongs to the general culture of France? Probably not. Critics who wrote about him were almost always specialists in English literature. The translations from his poetry were representative and satisfactory, but as his work was never translated in full, a considerable part of it remains, to many readers, inaccessible. For the general public he is a name—the Poet Laureate. At most —and this applies especially to the period after 1885 when he was recognised as a classic by the University of Paris— he is remembered as the author of *Enoch Arden* and the *Idylls of the King*. This renown is credited to him, he is celebrated without being read. But, after all, how many English poets since Byron have enjoyed even this modest fortune among the French public? Edmond Scherer, in the tenth volume of his *Études critiques*, refers to the surprise and amusement caused among Parisians by the list, published in the *Pall Mall Gazette*, of the forty eminent Englishmen who might be held to correspond to the forty of the French Academy. "Except for Lord Salisbury and Mr. Gladstone, and Tennyson the Poet Laureate, people heard these names for the first time. Let us except also Browning and Swinburne, about whom it was known more or less vaguely that they wrote poetry. . . . But Matthew Arnold, Jowett, Huxley, George Meredith, who in the world might they be?" Thus Tennyson's name was more widely known than that of any of his contemporaries, but his work very little.[1]

[1] M. Valéry Larbaud suggests that the resemblance between his name and the word "tennis" helped to make it familiar to the unlettered; he adds that the character in Joyce's *Ulysses* who refers to Lawn-Tennyson is making a joke which is as French as it is Irish.

About the more restricted public of the cultured one can say little with certainty. Spheres of influence are many, and we lack information as to the fortunes in France of many of the poets concerned.[1] Although Shelley was 'rediscovered' comparatively late, and translated in full, it is hard to believe that his influence exceeded Tennyson's. The same applies to the Pre-Raphaelite poets, whose vogue was perhaps wider, but very brief.[2] Swinburne influenced the *fin de siècle* poets more, perhaps, than Tennyson, but his is a special case, as he himself owed more than he gave to France. The influence in France of Keats and Browning sems to have been negligible.

It is curious that Tennyson should have had any importance for France at all, since he was far more a national than a world figure.[3] He did not enter European literature at a critical moment. His genius was not of a creative kind: he did not take men's minds and imaginations by storm like Byron. His poetry was an individual cult of beauty; it closed an age. His influence, infinitely less important than Byron's, made its way imperceptibly; or perhaps it would be more accurate to say that certain poets

[1] R. de Gourmont in the 1st series of *Promenades littéraires* (*La Littérature anglaise en France*) declares that since Sainte-Beuve's dealings with the Lake poets, no English poet—neither Swinburne, Browning, nor Tennyson—has had much influence in France.

[2] Mary Darmesteter (art. quoted, 1892) says: "Among poets of the Latin Quarter we should find many adepts of Pre-Raphaelitism for a single one who has read *In Memoriam* or the fluid music of *Idylls of the King*". On the other hand, Edmond Pilon in his centenary article considers that Tennyson's influence "far exceeded that of the legendary and Pre-Raphaelite vogue".

[3] One notes, for example, that M. André Chevrillon in his study of *La Pensée de Ruskin* (1909) constantly has recourse to quotations from Tennyson in order to sum up some trait in the English character, to indicate some essentially English attitude or state of mind. M. Cazamian in *L'Angleterre moderne* (Paris, Alcan, 1911) shows that in Tennyson's work there is a characteristically English reconciliation of liberalism with traditionalism.

turned towards Tennyson, and that from the diversity of his poetry, subordinated as it all was to the same ideal of beauty and purity, each drew the inspiration he needed. First, certain poets who stood in some relationship to the Parnassian movement without belonging to it, or who even contested its supremacy, were indebted to Tennyson. Joseph Autran, in his rustic poetry, took something from the English Idylls, André Theuriet something from the imaginative ballad poems. Baudelaire, Verlaine, and Mallarmé all felt Tennyson's charm. Bourget was fascinated by the melancholy beauty that he found in Tennyson. Through Bourget and the critics who made literary explorations across the Channel Tennyson was made familiar to the young Symbolist poets, of whom many were in direct touch with English literature. Thus Tennyson's poetry had its share in that renaissance of idealism which took place in France about 1885, and which, in order to break the power of naturalism, found allies in Wagner's music, Pre-Raphaelite art, and in all the fantasy and mystery of English poetry. In that movement, in heroic figures of knights, in lovely, symbolic figures of ladies—like Elaine, Vivien, the Lady of Shalott—we find traces of Tennyson. He brought to it a high idealism more in touch with common humanity than that of Wagner: his idealism helped to free French poetry from the bonds of positivism.

BIBLIOGRAPHY

STANDARD EDITION OF TENNYSON'S WORKS

The Works of Tennyson: annotated by Alfred Lord Tennyson. Edited by Hallam Lord Tennyson. (The Eversley Edition.) 9 volumes (Macmillan), 1908.

For the bibliography of Tennyson's Works, see

The Cambridge History of English Literature (Cambridge University Press, 1916), vol. xiii. pp. 473-479.

Alfred Lord Tennyson: A Memoir by his Son. Hallam Lord Tennyson (Macmillan, 1897), vol. i. pp. xviii-xxii— *Chronology of the books of poems.*

ENGLISH TEXTS OF TENNYSON PUBLISHED IN FRANCE[1]

Les Idylles du Roi: Enoch Arden. Introduction et notes par A. Baret. Paris (Garnier), 1886, in-18.

Enoch Arden: Les Idylles du Roi (éd. P. Sevrette). Paris (Vve. Bélin), 1887, in-12.

Enoch Arden: texte anglais annoté par M. l'abbé Courtois, Paris (Poussielgue), 1888, in-16. 2nd ed. 1891. 3rd ed. 1893. 4th ed. 1899.

Enoch Arden: texte anglais avec une notice sur la vie et les œuvres de Tennyson, par A. Beljame. Paris (Hachette), 1892, petit in-16. 8 editions appeared before 1909.

Tennyson: Quatre Poèmes. The Lotus-Eaters. Ulysses. The Brook. Enoch Arden. Texte anglais publié avec une notice sur la vie et les œuvres de Tennyson. Par G. Vallod. Paris (Hachette), 1908, in-16. 2nd ed. (*id.*), 1911, in-16.

---

[1] These are all scholastic editions.

Enoch Arden. The Brook. Ulysses. The Lotos-Eaters. With an English commentary by P. Lestang. Marseille (Ferran jeune), 1904, in-12. 2nd ed. (*id.*), 1908, in-16. 3rd ed. (*id.*), 1914, in-16.

TRANSLATIONS OF TENNYSON

IDYLLS OF THE KING.

Énide: traduit en prose française par Francisque Michel, avec neuf gravures sur acier d'après Gustave Doré. Paris (Hachette), 1867, in-folio.

Viviane: traduit en prose française par Francisque Michel, avec neuf gravures sur acier d'après Gustave Doré. Paris (Hachette), 1868, in-folio.

Élaine: traduit en prose française par Francisque Michel, avec neuf gravures sur acier d'après Gustave Doré. Paris (Hachette), 1868, in-folio.

Genièvre: traduit en prose française par Francisque Michel, avec neuf gravures sur acier d'après Gustave Doré. Paris (Hachette), 1869, in-folio.

Les Idylles du Roi: traduites en prose française par Francisque Michel, avec 36 gravures sur acier d'après Gustave Doré. Paris (Hachette), 1869, in-folio.

In Reviews:

Pelléas et Ettarre: prose translation by Amédée Pichot, *Revue britannique*, April 1870.

Le Trépas d'Arthur: literal translation in prose by Olivier Georges Destrée, *La Société Nouvelle*, August 1891.

ENOCH ARDEN.

Essais de traduction: Tennyson, Longfellow (Enoch Arden), par Lucien de La Rive. Paris (Ch. Meyrueis), 1870, in-12.

Enoch Arden, interprétation en vers, par E. Blémont (Bibliothèque du Progrès artistique et littéraire), 1885. First appeared serially in *Le Progrès artistique et littéraire*, 1885: reproduced in *Beautés étrangères* by E. Blémont. Paris (Lemerre), 1904, in-12.

Enoch Arden, poème, traduit par Xavier Marmier. Paris (Lemerre), 1887, in-16. This translation first appeared in the *Revue britannique*, July 1877.

Enoch Arden, Ulysse, Locksley Hall: traduits par Albert Buisson du Berger. Paris (Bibliothèque populaire Gautier, 1888), in-12.

Enoch Arden: traduit par l'Abbé Courtois. Paris (Poussielgue), 1888. 2nd ed. 1890. 3rd ed. 1897. 6th ed. 1909.

Enoch Arden: traduit par Émile Duglin. Beauvais(Drubay), 1889, in-8.

Enoch Arden: traduit en prose française par A. Beljame. Paris (Hachette), 1892, in-16.

Enoch Arden: traduit avec le texte anglais en regard par A. Beljame. Paris (Hachette), 1892, in-16. (5th ed. 1909).

In Reviews:

Enoch Arden: traduit en prose française par P. M., *Revue de Paris*, August 15, 1868.

MAUD.

Maud: préface et traduction par Henri Fauvel. Le Havre (Lemale), 1892, in-12.

IN MEMORIAM.

In Memoriam: traduit en vers français par Léon Morel. Paris (Hachette), 1898, in-16. 2nd ed., (*id.*) 1909, in-12.

SELECTED POEMS.

Poèmes divers d'Alfred Tennyson: traduits en vers français par Léon Morel. Paris (Hachette), 1899, in-16.

TENNYSON'S DRAMAS.

Marie Tudor: drame de Tennyson, traduit et mis en vers par E. Rastoul. Avignon (F. Séguin), 1908, in-16.

Le Faucon: saynète en un acte, traduite et mise en vers par E. Rastoul. Avignon (F. Séguin), 1907, in-16.

Thomas Becket: drame de Tennyson traduit et mis en vers par E. Rastoul. Avignon (F. Séguin), 1907, in-16.

STUDIES OF TENNYSON

I. IN PERIODICALS[1]

Anon.: Alfred Tennyson, *L'Europe littéraire*, Mar. 6 and 15, 1833.

Anon.: Alfred Tennyson, *Le Voleur*, Dec. 20, 1834.

*E. D. FORGUES: Alfred Tennyson, *Revue des Deux Mondes*, May 1, 1847.

*J. MILSAND: Alfred Tennyson, *Revue des Deux Mondes*, July 15, 1851.

L. ÉTIENNE: Alfred Tennyson, *Revue contemporaine*, vol. vi. Feb. and Mar. 1853.

*E. MONTÉGUT: Des premiers poèmes aux Idylles du roi, *Revue des Deux Mondes*, Nov. 1859.

J. L. M.: Un poème de Tennyson, *Bibliothèque universelle*, Sept. 1860.

*H. TAINE: Tennyson, *Journal des Débats*, Apr. 3, 4, 6, 1861.

A. RENAUD: Alfred Tennyson, *Revue contemporaine*, vol. xxxv. 1863.

A. VERMOREL: Enoch Arden, *Revue de Paris*, nouvelle série, Sept. 1864.

*H. GOMONT: Tennyson, *Revue de l'Est*, Jan. 1865.

Anon.: Alfred Tennyson, ses derniers poèmes, *Bibliothèque universelle*, Apr.-May 1865.

A. RENAUD: Enoch Arden, *Revue contemporaine*, Jan. 1866.

*E. MONTÉGUT: Enoch Arden et les poèmes populaires, *Revue des Deux Mondes*, Mar. 1866.

E. SCHERER: Alfred Tennyson, *Le Temps*, Jan. 11, 1870.

E. BLÉMONT: Tennyson, *La Renaissance artistique et littéraire*, May 11, 1872.

L. BOUCHER: Les Drames de Tennyson, *La Revue des Deux Mondes*, Apr. 15, 1876.

A. FILON: Lord Tennyson, *La Revue des Deux Mondes*, Sept. 1, 1885.

---

[1] Review articles are noted first as showing most clearly the spread of knowledge of Tennyson in France. * Indicates articles afterwards reprinted in book form, and which are therefore most accessible. See II.

BIBLIOGRAPHY

A. JAMES: Tennyson et Gladstone, *La Société nouvelle*, tome i. 1887.

H. JACOTTET: Tennyson, *Bibliothèque universelle*, Mar.-May 1888.

*G. SARRAZIN: Tennyson, *Nouvelle Revue*, Dec. 15, 1888.

F. DE P.: Tennyson, *Le Temps*, Oct. 7, 1892.

J. ST. CÈRE: Tennyson, *Le Figaro*, Oct. 7, 1892.

C. H. FORMENTIN: Tennyson chez Stéphane Mallarmé, *Écho de Paris*, Oct. 8, 1892.

DE BLOWITZ: Le poète-lauréat, *Le Gaulois*, Oct. 7, 1892.

*T. DE WYZEWA: Tennyson, *Le Figaro*, Oct. 9, 1892.

A. FILON: Lord Tennyson, *Le Journal des Débats*, Oct. 11, 1892.

A. THEURIET: Alfred Tennyson, *Le Journal*, Oct. 17, 1892.

G. STEIGLER: Qui remplacera Tennyson? *Écho de Paris*, Oct. 18, 1892.

MARY DARMESTETER, Tennyson, *Revue bleue*, Nov. 12, 1892.

F. LOLIÉE: Les disparus, Alfred Tennyson, *Nouvelle Revue*, Nov. 1892.

*S. MALLARMÉ: Tennyson vu d'ici, *National Observer*, Oct. 24, 1892; *Revue blanche*, Dec. 1892.

M. BOUCHOR: Becket, de Tennyson, *Revue hebdomadaire*. Mar. 11, 1893.

*C. LOOTEN: Alfred Tennyson, *Revue de Lille*, Jan.-Apr. 1893.

A. FILON: Les drames de Tennyson, *Revue des Deux Mondes*, Aug. 1895.

G. VALBERT (V. CHERBULIEZ): La vie d'Alfred, Lord Tennyson, *Revue des Deux Mondes*, Dec. 1, 1897.

M. DRONSART: Lord Tennyson, *Le Correspondant*, Nov. 10, Dec. 10, 1897.

A. BARTHÉLEMY: Tennyson, *Revue hebdomadaire*, Mar. 1898.

H. D. DAVRAY: La biographie d'Alfred, Lord Tennyson, *L'Ermitage*, Dec. 1900.

M. DUTOIT: La vie de Tennyson, *Revue des jeunes filles*, Feb. 1900.

C. DESSOMMES: Un poète heureux, *Revue de Paris*, Feb. 15, 1901.

Ch. Déjob: Les Pauvres Gens de Victor Hugo et Enoch Arden, *Revue des Cours et des Conférences* (p. 751), 1900.

H. Brémond: Le Centenaire de Tennyson, *Le Correspondant*, July 15, 1909.

E. Faguet: The Centenary of Tennyson, *Quarterly Review*, Apr. 1909.

*F. Roz: Tennyson, *Revue des Deux Mondes*, Aug. 5, 1909.

*E. Pilon: Alfred Tennyson, *Écho de Paris*, Aug. 6, 1909.

G. Grappe: Alfred Tennyson, *L'Opinion*, Aug. 7, 1909.

Anon.: Le Centenaire de Tennyson, *Le Temps*, Aug. 11, 1909.

H. D. Davray: Alfred Tennyson, *Mercure de France*, Aug. 16, 1909.

J. Lux: Le Centenaire de Tennyson, *Revue bleue*, Aug. 21, 1909.

A. Filon: Le Centenaire de Tennyson à Oxford, *Journal des Débats*, Sept. 29, 1909.

E. Dupuy: Alfred Tennyson, le poète-lauréat, *Revue hebdomadaire*, Jan. 1915.

II. In Books

H. Gomont: Tennyson (poètes anglais du XIXe siècle). Metz, 1865, in-8.

Le P. Ragey: Tennyson. Paris (Delhomme), 1899, in-16.

C. Looten: Une Biographie de Tennyson. Arras (Sueur-Charruey), 1900, in-8.

F. Roz: Tennyson. Paris (Bloud), 1911, in-12.

E. D. Forgues: Originaux et beaux-esprits de l'Angleterre. Paris (Charpentier), 1860, in-16.

H. Taine: Histoire de la littérature anglaise, tome iv. ch. vi., Paris (Hachette), 1864, in-8.

V. Laprade: Le Sentiment de la nature chez les modernes. Paris (Didier), 1867, in-8.

C. Barot: Histoire de la littérature contemporaine en Angleterre, 1830–1874. Paris (Charpentier), 1874, in-12.

M. Formont: Du roman en vers. Bar-sur-Aube (Lebois), 1885, in-8.

E. Montégut: Écrivains modernes de l'Angleterre, tome ii. Paris (Hachette), 1889, in-12.

G. Sarrazin: La Renaissance de la poésie anglaise. Paris (Perrin), 1889, in-16.

J. Milsand: Littérature anglaise et philosophie. Paris (Fischbacher), 1893, in-8.

T. de Wyzewa: Écrivains étrangers. Paris (Perrin), 1896, in-16.

S. Mallarmé: Divagations. Paris (Fasquelle), 1897, in-12.

E. Pilon, Sites et personnages. Paris (Grasset), 1912, in-12.

J. Douady : La mer et les poètes anglais. Paris (Hachette), 1912, in-12.

BOOKS OF GENERAL INTEREST IN WHICH REFERENCE IS MADE TO TENNYSON IN FRANCE

E. Scherer: Études critiques sur la littérature contemporaine, vols. iv., vi., vii., x. Paris (Lévy), 1886–1889, in-12.

P. Bourget: Études et portraits. 2 vols. Paris (Lemerre), 1888, in-12.

H. Bérenger: L'Aristocratie intellectuelle. Paris (Colin), 1895, in-12.

J. Texte: Les Relations littéraires de la France avec l'étranger depuis 1848 (in *Histoire de la langue et de la littérature françaises* of Petit de Julleville), vol. 8. Paris (Colin), 1899, gd. in-8).

C. Mauclair: L'Art en silence. Paris (Ollendorf), 1901, in-18.

F. Brunetière: Études critiques VIIe série (Le mouvement littéraire européen au XIXe siècle). Paris (Hachette), 1903, in-16.

R. de Gourmont: Promenades littéraires Ière série (La littérature anglaise en France). Paris (Mercure de France), 1904, in-12.

F. C. Roe: Taine et l'Angleterre. Paris (Champion), 1923, in-8.

E. Partridge: The French Romantics' Knowledge of English Literature. Paris (Champion), 1924, in-80.

INFLUENCE

Joseph Autran: La Vie rurale. Paris (Michel Lévy), 1856, in-12.

C. Baudelaire: Les Fleurs du mal. Paris (Poulet-Malassis), 1857, in-12.

A. Theuriet: In Memoriam, *Revue des Deux Mondes*, Aug. 15, 1857.

F. Frank: Le Poème de la jeunesse. Paris (M. Lévy), 1876, in-16.

P. Bourget: Poésies, 1872–1876. Paris (Lemerre), 1876, in-16. Poésies, 1876–1882. Paris (Lemerre), 1882, in-16.

P. Verlaine: Sagesse. Paris (Palmé), 1881, in-8. Amour. Paris (Vanier), 1888, in-12. (Œuvres complètes, Messein, 1923, vols. i. et ii.)

J. Lorrain: La Forêt bleue. Paris (Lévy), 1883, in-12. L'ombre ardente. Paris (Fasquelle), 1897, in-12.

H. de Régnier: Poèmes anciens et romanesques, 1887–1889. Paris (Mercure de France), 1890.

H. Bérenger, L'Ame moderne. Paris (Perrin), 1892, in-16.

A. F. Hérold: Chevaleries sentimentales. Paris, 1893 (Lib. d'art indépendant).

A. Fontainas, Nuits d'épiphanies. Paris (Mercure de France), 1894, in-12.

S. Merrill, Poèmes, 1887–1897. Paris (Mercure de France), 1897, in-12.

E. Blémont, En mémoire d'un enfant. Paris (Lemerre), 1899, in-8 .

L. Le Cardonnel, Poèmes, Paris (Mercure de France), 1904, in-12.

INDEX

Adeline, 114
Aicard, Jean, 3
Album des Légendes, L', 120
Art et Critique, 108
Athenaeum, 66
Aubry, G. Jean, 103, 105 n.
Audley Court, 14 n., 15
Autran, Joseph, 48, 49, 153
Aylmer's Field, 94

Baignières, J., 114
Baldenne, Fernand, 51 n.
Ballads and Other Poems, 85
Banquet, Le, 114
Banville, Théodore de, 108, 109
Baudelaire, Charles, 92; Baudelaire and T., 100-102; 108, 109, 153
Becket, 144
Beljame, A, 76
Bentham, Jeremy, 8
Bérenger, Henry, 88, 92-94, 135
Bibliothèque universelle, 42-43, 44, 70
Blackwood's, 7
Blémont, Émile, 71-75, 113, 140-141
Bouchor, Maurice, 94-95
Bourget, Paul, 80, 88, 94-99, 116, 153.
Brémond, H., 137
Brizeux, Auguste, 48, 59
Brook, The, 52, 54, 94
Browning, E. B., 43, 93
Browning, Robert, 19, 21, 40, 132, 151, 152
Brunetière, Ferdinand, 30
Buisson du Berger, A., 74, 76
Burne-Jones, 116, 135
Byron, Lord, 3, 8, 11, 13, 19, 50, 53, 92, 102, 137; fame in France, 150-152

Carlyle, Thomas, 33
Chasles, Philarète, 12
Châtelain, Chevalier de, 52-53
Cherbuliez, Victor, 136

Chevrillon, André, 32, 88, 117, 119
Circumstance, 14 n., 15
Claribel, 54
Constable, John, 17
Constitutionnel, Le, 63
Coppée, François, 3, 31, 78, 87, 150
Coulon, Marcel, 103 n., 111
Courtois, Abbé, 75
Crossing the Bar, 142
Cunningham, Allan, 10, 11

Darmesteter, James, 129
Darmesteter, Mme. (Mary Robinson), 131-132
Davray, H. D., 136
Death of the Old Year, 9, 135
Demeter, 133
Dernière Mode, La, 56
Deserted House, The, 135
Destrée, O. G., 113, 114, 135
Dora, 14, 48, 49
Doré, Gustave, 60-64, 133
Doumic, René, 120
Duglin, É., 76
Dujardin, Édouard, 115
Dying Swan, The, 113

Eagle, The, 52 n.
Écho de la Littérature et des Beaux-Arts, 13
Écho de Paris, 129, 133
Elaine, 43, 53, 60
Eleonore, 11, 114
Elliott, Ebenezer, 10, 11
Enoch Arden, 24, 37, 55, 60; fortune of, 66-80; 85, 86, 133, 137, 150, 151
Europe littéraire, L', 8-9

Faguet, Émile, 146, 147, 148
Falcon, The, 144
Fauvel, Henri, 80-83
Feuillet, Octave, 94 n., 130

Figaro, Le, 130, 132
Filon, Augustin, 85, 87, 88, 89-90; *Amours anglais,* 94; 130, 131, 139, 146
FitzGerald, Edward, 12
Fontainas, André, 124-125
Forgues, E. D., 16-18, 21
France, Anatole, 94
Frank, Félix, 46

Gaulois, Le, 131
Gazette des Beaux-Arts, La, 116
Ghéon, H., 109
Godiva, 14
Goethe, 39
Gomont, H. de, 53-54
Goose, The, 54
Gosse, Edmund, 3, 146
Grandmother, The, 24, 37, 86, 87
Grappe, Georges, 147
Guérin, Charles, 141, 142 n.

Hallam, Arthur, 7, 12
Heine, 92
Hennequin, Émile, 92
Hérold, A. Ferdinand, 124
Holy Grail, The, 38, 54
Hugo, Victor, 2, 3, 43, 77, 84, 92, 107, 115, 119, 147
Hunt, Leigh, 7

Idylls of the King, 25, 29, 30, 37, 40, 43, 44, 53, 59; translation of, 60-66, 75, 86, 87, 89, 90, 91, 98, 119, 131, 133, 135, 142, 151
In Memoriam, 18, 19, 21, 22, 23, 25, 27, 28, 36, 40, 44, 47, 52, 53, 54, 84, 86, 87, 89, 105, 106, 107, 134; Morel's translation, 138-140, 142

Journal, Le, 130
Journal de littérature étrangère, Le, 8
Journal des Débats, Le, 24, 65, 130, 139
Juvenilia, 86

Kahn, Gustave, 117
Keats, 17, 42, 152
Ker, W. P., 145

Lacaussade, A., 42
Lady Clara Vere de Vere, 16
Lady Clare, 14 n., 15, 47
Lady of Shalott, The, 54 n., 113, 125
Lamartine, 42; *Jocelyn,* 48-49, 77, 78; 92

Lanson, Gustave, 51, 140
Laprade, Victor de, 49, 50-51, 84
Larbaud, Valéry, 149-150
Le Cardonnel, Louis, 126-127, 135
Livre des Légendes, Le, 120
Locksley Hall, 19, 23, 25, 27, 46, 91, 92, 93, 96, 113, 134, 143
Locksley Hall Sixty Years after, 86
Longfellow, 42, 100
Looten, C., 130, 138
Lord of Burleigh, The, 14
Lorrain, Jean, 116-119, 135
Lotos-Eaters, The, 39, 53, 100, 113, 114, 134
Love and Death, 14, 15, 52 n.
Lucas, H., 44, 45
Lucretius, 55, 68

Mallarmé, Stéphane, 4, 56-57, 65, 73, 80, 111-113, 117, 120, 129; *Tennyson vu d'ici,* 133-134; 136, 153
Margaret, 114
Mariana, 16, 39, 44, 45, 46, 52 n., 53, 56-57, 99, 113
Marmier, X., 55, 69, 76
Mauclair, Camille, 111, 112
Maud, 22, 23, 25, 27, 28, 30, 40, 59; translation of, 80-83; 85, 86, 89, 91, 93, 94, 96-97, 102, 114, 133; *Maud,* xxii., translation of, 133
Mercure de France, 113, 135, 145
Meredith, George, 112
Mermaid, The, 16
Merman, The, 135
Merrill, Stuart, 120, 122-124
Michel, Francisque, 60, 63
Mill, J. S., 7
Miller's Daughter, The, 37, 94
Milsand, Joseph, 19-20, 21
Montégut, Émile, 23, 33-38, 76, 85, 86
Moore, George, 104
Moore, Thomas, 3, 11
Morel, Léon, 138-140, 142-144
Morice, Charles, 98, 105 n.
Morris, William, 59
Morte d'Arthur, 16
Mourey, Gabriel, 88, 117
Mouvement littéraire, Le, 65
Musset, Alfred de, 2, 3; Taine's comparison of Tennyson and Musset, 31-32; 40

Nation, The, 146
Nicolson, Harold, 1
North, Christopher, 7

INDEX

Northern Farmer, The, 24, 37, 78
Nouvelle Revue, La, 114, 130
Nouvelle Revue française, La, 109
Nouvelle Revue de Paris, La, 55

Ode on the Death of the Duke of Wellington, 147
Oenone, 53, 134, 135, 143

Pall Mall Gazette, 151
Passing of Arthur, The, 113, 123
Pelleas and Ettarre, 54, 96
Pichot, Amédée, 13, 14, 16, 54
Pilon, Edmond, 146, 147
Plume, La, 92, 113, 135
Poe, E. A., 56, 95, 100, 101, 102, 109, 111, 112, 113
Poems by Two Brothers, 8
Poems, Chiefly Lyrical, 7
Poet, The, 14, 15, 92
Poizat, Alfred, 121
Pre-Raphaelites, The, 89, 98; Pre-Raphaelite illustrators of Tennyson, 116-117; influence in France, 152-153
Princess, The, 22, 25, 28, 29, 30, 40, 98, 99, 122-123, 142
Progrès artistique et littéraire, 72
Puvis de Chavannes, 133

Quarterly, The, 7, 44, 146
Queen Mary, 144
Quinet, Edgar, 59

Ragey, Le Père, 137-138
Rastoul, Édouard, 144
Recollections of the Arabian Nights, 9, 114
Régnier, Henri de, 120-122
Renaissance artistique et littéraire, La, 71
Renaud, Armand, 67, 101 n.
Revue bleue, La, 132, 146
Revue britannique, La, 13, 14, 15, 19, 21, 22, 42, 44, 54, 55, 67, 69
Revue contemporaine, Lo, 20, 67, 89
Revue de l'Est, La, 53
Revue de Lille, La, 130
Revue de l'Instruction publique, La, 63, 64
Revue de Paris, La, 9, 10, 20, 67
Revue des Deux Mondes, La, 10, 16, 23, 33, 45, 85
Revue européenne, La, 43, 44
Revue française, La, 42
Revue générale, La, 135
Revue hebdomadaire, La, 135

Revue indépendante, La, 57, 92, 113
Revue wagnérienne, La, 115
Rimbaud, Arthur, 103
Ring out, wild bells, 44
Rive, Lucien de la, 69
Rizpah, 86, 89, 142
Rod, Édouard, 88, 89
Rossetti, D. G., 117
Rothenstein, W., 107
Roz, Firmin, 146, 147, 148

St. Agnes Eve, 14
Saint-Germain, J. T. de, 47
Saint-Graal, Le, 120
St. Simon Stylites, 14
Sarrazin, Gabriel, 88, 90-92, 99
Schérer, Edmond, 38-41, 71, 84-85, 89, 151
Schuré, Édouard, 126
Shakespeare, 38, 43, 84, 99, 108, 150
Shelley, 12, 17, 31, 34, 53, 88, 89, 92, 98, 99; influence in France, 152
Signoret, Emmanuel, 120
Silent Voices, The, 142
Sisters, The, 14 n., 15
Sleeping Palace, The, 116
Société Nouvelle, La, 113
Southey, 11
Spenser, 12, 131
Swinburne, A. C., 3, 4, 28, 31, 32, 112, 113, 124, 151; influence in France, 152
Symons, Arthur, 106, 107, 109

Taine, H., 24-33, 50, 64, 71, 80, 84, 85, 86, 89, 91, 92, 98, 131, 133, 147
Talking Oak, The, 54 n., 94
Tardieu, J., 47
Tears, idle tears, 51, 95, 99
Tellier, Jules, 80, 87, 97
Temps, Le, 38, 71, 131, 145
Tennyson, Alfred, Lord, Relations with France, 2-6; early French notices of his work and first translations, 7-18; comments on Laureateship, 18-23; Taine's judgment on, 24-33; Montégut and T., 33-38; Scherer on T., 38-41; indications of French knowledge of T., 42-45; influence on Theuriet and others, 45-48; Laprade on T.'s Nature poetry, 49-50; various translations, 51-56; Mallarmé's version of *Mariana*, 56-57; fortune of the *Idylls of the King*, 60-66;

Enoch Arden, translations, 67-76; influence of, 78-80; *Maud*, translation, 80-83; evolution of criticism, 84-94; T. and Bourget, 94-99; T. and Baudelaire, 100-102; T. and Verlaine, 102-111; T. and Mallarmé, 111-113; T. in the Symbolist reviews, 113-115; cult of legendary poetry, T.'s influence on various Symbolist poets, 115-128; judgments on T. at his death, 129-135; biographies of T., 135-138; Morel's translation of *In Memoriam*, 138-140; influence of *In Memoriam*, 140-141; translations by Morel, *Poèmes divers*, 142-144; translation of dramas, 144; centenary judgments on T., 144-148; T.'s fortune in France, 149-151
Tennyson, Hallam Lord, 3, 136
Texte, J., 99
Theuriet, André, 45-46, 48, 78-80, 130, 153
Thibaudet, A., 111, 112
Thome, A., 108

Times, The, 66, 67
Tiresias and other Poems, 85
Tolstoy, 87
Two Voices, The, 16, 53

Ulysses, 39

Verlaine, Paul, and England, 102-104; Verlaine and *In Memoriam*, 105-107; T. and Verlaine's lyricism, 108-111; 115, 128, 153
Vielé-Griffin, Francis, 107, 108, 121, 122
Villemarqué, H. de la, 60
Voleur, Le, 11

Wagner, 87, 111, 115, 116, 120, 124, 131, 153
Warren, Sir Herbert, 144-145, 150
Westminster Review, 7, 8
Whitman, Walt, 93, 113
Wordsworth, 17, 34, 88, 98
Wyzewa, Téodor de, 132

Yeats, W. B., 106

Zola, Émile, 87

MANCHESTER UNIVERSITY
French Series

LES ŒUVRES DE GUIOT DE PROVINS. Poète Lyrique et Satirique. Edited by JOHN ORR, M.A. 8vo. 10*s*. 6*d*. net. (No. I.)

ŒUVRES POETIQUES DE JEAN DE LINGENDES. Edited by E. T. GRIFFITHS, M.A. Crown 8vo. 7*s*. 6*d*. net. (No. II.)

THE TEACHING AND CULTIVATION OF THE FRENCH LANGUAGE IN ENGLAND DURING TUDOR AND STUART TIMES. With an Introductory Chapter on the Preceding Period. By KATHLEEN LAMBLEY, M.A. 8vo. 14*s*. net. (No. III.)

LE LAI D'HAVELOC AND GAIMAR'S HAVELOC EPISODE. Edited by ALEXANDER BELL, M.A. Crown 8vo. 7*s*. 6*d*. net. (No. IV.)

MANCHESTER UNIVERSITY PRESS
23 LIME GROVE, OXFORD ROAD, MANCHESTER

MANCHESTER UNIVERSITY
English Series

THE LITERARY PROFESSION IN THE ELIZABETHAN AGE. By PHŒBE SHEAVYN, M.A., D.Litt. 8vo. 7s. 6d. net.

BEOWULF: Edited, with Introduction, Bibliography, Notes, Glossary, and Appendixes, by W. J. SEDGEFIELD, Litt.D. 8vo. 9s. net. *Second Edition.*

PATIENCE: A West Midland Poem of the Fourteenth Century. Edited, with Introduction, Bibliography, Notes, and Glossary, by HARTLEY BATESON, B.A. Crown 8vo. 6s. net. *Second Edition.*

THE EARLY LIFE OF GEORGE ELIOT. By MARY H. DEAKIN, M.A. With an Introductory Note by C. H. HERFORD, Litt.D. 8vo. 6s. net.

THE POETICAL WORKS OF WILLIAM DRUMMOND OF HAWTHORNDEN. To which is added A CYPRESSE GROVE. Edited by L. E. KASTNER, M.A. With Illustrations. 2 vols. 16s. net.

THOMAS HARDY. A Study of the Wessex Novels. Second Edition, with an Appendix on The Poems and The Dynasts. By H. C. DUFFIN, M.A. Crown 8vo. 7s. 6d. net.

THE POETICAL WORKS OF SIR WILLIAM ALEXANDER, EARL OF STIRLING. Edited by L. E. KASTNER, Litt.D., and H. B. CHARLTON, M.A. 8vo.
Vol. I. The Dramatic Works. With an Introductory Essay on the Growth of the Senecan Tradition in Renaissance Tragedy. 28s. net.
Vol. II. 25s. net.

GEORGE GISSING: An Appreciation. By MAY YATES, M.A. Crown 8vo. 6s. net.

THE MONKS AND THE GIANTS. By J. HOOKHAM FRERE. Edited, with Notes and an Introduction on the Italian Medley Poets and their English Imitators, by R. D. WALLER, M.A. Crown 8vo. 7s. 6d. net.

AN ANGLO-SAXON BOOK OF VERSE AND PROSE. By W. J. SEDGEFIELD, M.A., Litt.D. 8vo. 12s. 6d. net.

AN ANGLO-SAXON VERSE BOOK *from the above.* 7s. 6d. net.

AN ANGLO-SAXON PROSE BOOK *from the above.* 7s. 6d. net.

MANCHESTER UNIVERSITY PRESS
23 LIME GROVE, OXFORD ROAD, MANCHESTER

3-31-66